Cast Iron

From Stove to Table, Quick & Easy, Everyday Cast Iron Recipes

Louise Davidson

ISBN: 978-1979329569

Printed in the United States

Contents

Introduction

The cast iron cookware is something that many of our grandmothers have been using for a long time, and it can be found only by digging quite a bit through the old stuff in the kitchen. Once found like that, the impression it gives off at first is probably that it looks like something that would require time and muscle to use and maintain, as its appearance is surely not all sleek and elegant.

However, you'll soon find yourself preparing some of the best, juiciest, most delicious steaks on that "old thing", all the while thinking of how oblivious you were as to how precious an heirloom the cast iron pan actually is.

The number of dishes one can cook and the easiness in doing so with the the cast iron pan is amazing. They also turn out delicious and cleaning up is a breeze. Yes, the cast iron pan is truly ancient, having been with us for centuries. But it's no wonder it's still around. Its durability makes it versatile. You can use it to make steaks, soups and stews on the stovetop or roast, grill and bake in an oven.

This cookbook introduces many recipes that won't be able to not love. Aside from steaks, there are hearty, one-pot power breakfasts, pilafs, paellas, heavy dishes, light snacks, marvelous vegetarian fare and even decadent desserts!

Many of these recipes you'll find in this cookbook have as much of a tradition and refinement as you'd expect. You'll also be able to learn about the cast iron pan's history as well as pointers on how to care for it so you always get the best results. The cast iron itself lends a rustic decorative appeal in this age of shiny, modern cookware. See your guests' eyes open in amazement when it's placed on the dining table, straight from the oven!

I have no doubt you will fall in love with the cast iron pan just as I have. It's time to experiment and discover, innovate and create.

Grab your cast iron pan and let's begin!

What Is a Cast Iron Pan?

The cast iron pan is one of the sturdiest cooking pans you'll ever come across. It has been with us a long time. It can withstand and evenly distribute very high heat. This results in stronger flavor – flavor you can't get from cooking in a non-stick pan – and shorter cooking time.

Unlike modern pans which are made non-stick by synthetic linings, cast iron pans or skillets can be treated or "seasoned" to become non-stick naturally. The cast iron pan adsorbs flavors every time it's used, giving dishes richer, more complex flavor. This pan can last a lifetime – as long as it's treated right. It's something that you can pass down to your children and grandchildren.

A Bit of History

Anything made by pouring molten iron into a mold is called cast iron. Cast iron was first used way back around 513 BC. The technology originated in China, where it was used for making cookware and weapons. By around 1100 AD, it was being used to make pots in England. By the 15th century, it was used to make cannons.

When stovetops where invented in the 1700s and food no longer needed to be cooked outdoors over an open fire, cookware technology began to advance rapidly. Abraham Darby came up with a way to produce pots and kettles that were made from thinner cast iron and were more suitable for use in homes rather than outdoors. Around this time, George Washington's mother even included her cast iron pan in her will.

By the 1800s cast iron was widely used, giving rise to still-popular name brands such as Wagner, Griswold and Lodge.

Lately, questions are arising regarding the effects of chemicals used in modern cookware. This has led to renewed interest and popularity for the cast iron pan.

The Benefits

Love to Last a Lifetime

The cast iron pan is known for its durability. Rust or scratches can be repaired. This is something that could last a lifetime, as long as you use it properly. It can even be handed down for the next generation to enjoy.

Naturally Non-Stick

You get a convenient non-stick surface without harmful chemicals, simply iron and oil.

Leaner Fare

With a natural non-stick surface, you won't need as much oil or fat for cooking dishes in a cast iron pan. You'll be enjoying leaner yet tastier fare.

From Stovetop to Oven

It's durable enough to be used over open fire, on the stovetop and in the oven. Just imagine everything you can whip up without changing pans.

A Decorative Touch

The rustic and natural vintage look of the cast iron pan can add a more interesting and visually appealing touch to a table setting.

Iron Boost

Cooking in a cast iron pan can actually boost your iron intake, particularly if you use it to prepare acidic dishes like applesauce and pasta with tomato sauce. You get enough iron to meet your requirements without reaching toxic levels.

Ways You Can Cook with a Cast Iron Pan

Sear, Sauté and Stir-Fry

With a well-seasoned cast iron pan, you can cook over high heat without any sticking. Unlike non-stick pans, which can't be used over high heat, you can sear and brown foods well with a cast iron pan. After sautéing or stir-frying over the stovetop, you can immediately put it in the oven without having to change pans.

Bake

Cast iron retains and distributes heat evenly, and this is ideal for baking. Cakes baked in it have a noticeably rich, browned, good-textured crust. It can also serve as both the baking pan and the serving dish.

Braise

Cast iron maintains both high and low heat very well. This makes it able to keep heat even and stable for simmering. It's ideal for cooking cuts of meat that need to be cooked gently for long periods to soften.

Fry

Unlike other pans, which lose heat when food is added to hot oil, a cast iron pan can keep the heat constant. You get crispier exteriors and juicier interiors in fried food.

Seasoning a Cast Iron Pan

Seasoning a cast iron pan has two basic purposes:

1. To build a protective layer or patina over the surface that will protect it from damage such as rusting.
2. To make the pan naturally non-stick.

Most experienced cast iron pan users recommend seasoning both old and new pans, even those that are "pre-seasoned."

Here are the steps:
Note: For new pans, go straight to Step 3. Also, keep your kitchen well ventilated when seasoning your pan, as this process can cause the oil to smoke and produce an unpleasant odor.

1. Preheat the oven to 350°F.
2. Wash the whole skillet, including the handle and outer surface, with warm, soapy water and a sponge. Do not use steel wool, as this may scratch the pan and ruin it. Wash it thoroughly. It should be noted that this is the **only time** you use soapy water when cleaning cast iron!

3. Rinse the skillet with hot water and wipe it dry.
4. Place the skillet in the hot oven to dry. It should be completely dry. (You may also let it dry on the stovetop; just make sure that all moisture evaporates.)
5. Dip a paper towel in vegetable oil. Flaxseed oil is best, but you can use others like canola oil or coconut oil; you can even use lard.
6. Rub the oiled paper towel over the cast iron skillet to make a thick, even coat. You should cover both the inside and outside of the skillet. Use a clean, dry paper towel to remove any excess oil. Too much oil will leave the pan too sticky.
7. Place the cast iron skillet in the preheated oven, upside down and in the center. Place a baking sheet or aluminum foil underneath to catch any drips.
8. Bake for exactly an hour.
9. Turn off the oven, but leave the cast iron skillet inside.
10. Allow it to cool completely. Cast iron retains heat, so this will take time.
11. Wipe away any excess oil to leave a smooth, shiny skillet. You don't want puddles of oil in your pan.

And that is all you need to do. You can repeat the process whenever your skillet looks rusted or dull. General cooking, especially when using oil, will often keep the pan seasoned.

Taking Care of Your Pan

Seasoning twice a year is the best way to maintain your cast iron pan. It will keep your skillet in tip-top shape and help it last for a long time.

After use, immediately rinse the skillet by running hot water over it and wiping it to clean. To remove bits of stuck-on food, use a non-metal brush and scrub with coarse salt. This will help remove the food without wrecking the skillet. Sometimes, all you'll need is to wipe it clean using oil.

To avoid rust, always keep the pan dry. After washing, dry the skillet thoroughly. Drying with a towel is usually adequate, but if you live in an especially humid environment, dry it in the oven or let the moisture in the pan evaporate fully by heating over a stovetop. Leaving a cast iron skillet wet will cause rust to form, and this will shorten the life of your pan. If rust does form, use steel wool to remove it, but do not apply the steel wool to non-rusted parts of the skillet. After removing the rust, season the pan again.

Finally, spray your skillet with a small amount of cooking oil after each time you wash it. Place a paper towel inside the pan and store.

Proper care and maintenance of your cast iron pan will pay off as you will enjoy many years of using it. This means a lot of savings as well!

Other Helpful Pointers

Prepare in Advance

A cast iron pan retains heat so efficiently that you'll find the ingredients cooking more quickly than they would in an ordinary pan. It's best to have everything ready so you can take advantage of the retained heat and avoid burning because you were busy chopping the next ingredient.

Preheat Your Pan

Cast iron pans are great at retaining heat, but they can take a bit longer to heat up. There is, however, still some debate as to whether it's better to heat the pan before adding oil or to heat the pan along with the oil. Be extra careful when preheating on an electric range, as the heating coils may not heat up evenly and this could warp your pan. Use medium low to medium heat to preheat.

Choose the Pan You'll Need

For beginners, don't go buying a whole set in one go. The recipes here call for either a 10- or 12-inch pan. As the cast iron pan adsorbs aromas and flavors, you may eventually want to have one for savory dishes and another one for desserts.

Keep Safe

Always use oven mitts; the pan's handles will be as hot as the pan itself! Have other tools like tongs on hand to keep yourself safe from burns. An additional warning: Because a cast iron pan can heat up to a very high temperature, it could crack if cold water is suddenly added to it.

Choose the Right Oil

Although popular cooking oils are fine to use, remember that the skillet can take temperatures beyond the smoking point of many oils. Here are some oils that have high smoking points and will not degrade or produce smoke at high heat.

- Grape seed oil
- Peanut oil
- Palm oil
- Avocado oil

Keep Food in Containers

Leaving acidic ingredients like tomato sauce in a cast iron skillet will cause too much iron to leach out and blacken your food. Remove acidic food immediately after cooking and transfer to a storage container.

Experiment and Create Your Own Recipes

As you try out the following recipes, you'll become familiar with the basic procedures for preparing different dishes. Don't hesitate to try out your own ingredients and create your own recipes. You can start out by simply using your own substitutes for some of the ingredients. Very soon, you'll be able to develop your own techniques and secrets to using your cast iron pan.

Breakfast Recipes

Eggs with Crispy Potatoes and Green Beans

Serves: 4
Preparation Time: 5 minutes
Cooking Time: 20–25 minutes

Ingredients

1 cup fresh or cooked green beans, trimmed and cut into 1-inch pieces
2 Tablespoons extra-virgin olive oil
2 pounds raw or cooked potatoes, peeled and diced (½-inch cubes, if raw)
2 cloves garlic, minced
⅛ teaspoon red pepper flakes
½ teaspoon salt
Freshly ground pepper, to taste
4 large eggs, at room temperature
⅛ teaspoon paprika

Directions

1. Steam or blanch green beans. To blanch, drop into boiling water and cook until bright green and crisp (about 3 minutes). Rinse under cold water and drain.
2. Heat oil in cast iron skillet over medium heat. Oil is ready when a piece of potato dropped into it sizzles. Spread the potato slices over the skillet in a single layer. Cook, flipping over as needed, until tender inside and browned outside (about 15 minutes, or less if using cooked potato).
3. Stir in blanched green beans, garlic, red pepper flakes, salt and pepper.
4. Drop eggs over vegetables.
5. Cover and cook to desired doneness (about 3–5 minutes).
6. Sprinkle with paprika and serve.

Nutrition (per serving)

Calories 318
Carbs 42 g
Fat 12 g
Protein 12 g
Sodium 381 mg

Hash and Eggs

Serves: 1–2
Preparation Time: 10 minutes
Cooking Time: 20 minutes

Ingredients
1 small russet potato, scrubbed, unpeeled
1 slice bacon
1 Tablespoon extra-virgin olive oil
3 cups baby spinach
⅛ teaspoon salt
2 large eggs, at room temperature
⅔ cup shredded cheddar cheese
Freshly ground pepper

Directions
1. Prick potato all over and cook in the microwave on high (about 4 minutes). Let cool and dice.
2. Heat cast iron pan over medium high heat and cook bacon until crisp. Remove bacon and drain over paper towel.
3. Add oil to drippings in pan and cook diced potato until browned (about 5 minutes).
4. Add the spinach and cook until wilted.
5. Make two wells in the mixture and drop eggs in.
6. Season everything with salt.
7. Cover and reduce heat. Cook partially (about 2–3 minutes).
8. Sprinkle with cheese and replace cover. Cook until cheese is melted and eggs are done (about 1–2 minutes).
9. Sprinkle with chopped bacon and freshly ground black pepper.

Nutrition (per serving)
Calories 354
Carbs 25.5 g
Fat 21 g
Protein 17 g
Sodium 464 mg

Banana-Nut Quinoa

Serves: 6
Preparation Time: 10 minutes
Cooking Time: 25–30 minutes

Ingredients
3 Tablespoons coconut oil, divided
1 cup quinoa, rinsed
2 cups very hot water
¼ teaspoon salt
3 medium plantain bananas (or any firm and just ripened banana), sliced
½ cup dates, chopped
¼ cup shredded unsweetened coconut
1 teaspoon cinnamon

Topping:
2 Tablespoons brown sugar
1 teaspoon cinnamon
1 cup pecans or any nut or choice, toasted and coarsely chopped
½ cup fresh fruit of choice

Directions
1. Preheat oven to 375°F.
2. In a bowl, mix topping ingredients (except fresh fruit) together well and set aside.
3. In a cast iron skillet, heat 2 Tablespoons oil over medium heat.
4. Add bananas and cook until brown on both sides (about 3 minutes).
5. Transfer browned bananas to a plate. Set bananas and skillet aside.

6. In a small pot or saucepan, heat remaining oil over medium heat.
7. Stir in quinoa, coating well. Cook for 3 minutes.
8. Add hot water and salt.
9. Turn up heat to high and bring mixture to a boil.
10. Reduce heat and let simmer, covered, for 10 minutes.
11. After simmering, stir in dates, coconut, half the browned bananas, and cinnamon.
12. Transfer mixture to the skillet and spread evenly.
13. Scatter topping and remaining bananas over mixture.
14. Bake until golden brown (about 15–20 minutes, depending on size of skillet).
15. Serve with extra topping of fresh fruit.

Nutrition (per serving)
Calories 472
Carbs 60.9 g
Fat 25.6 g
Protein 7.0 g
Sodium 105 mg

Hearty Paleo Breakfast

Serves: 2–4
Preparation Time: 10 minutes
Cooking Time: 25 minutes

Ingredients
4 strips bacon, sugar-free, grass-fed and chopped
2 Tablespoons avocado oil
½ red onion, chopped
4 cloves garlic, minced
1 pound sugar-free pork breakfast sausage or beef burger
2 cups butternut squash, shredded
3 cups organic spinach
4 eggs, at room temperature
1 avocado, sliced
Green onions, chopped, for garnish

Directions
1. Heat the cast iron skillet over medium heat and cook bacon until browned.
2. Add oil and onion. Cook until onion is translucent (about 3–5 minutes).
3. Add garlic and sausage or hamburger mixture. Cook, stirring frequently, until browned (about 10 minutes).
4. Preheat broiler to high (about 5 minutes before you're ready to put skillet and ingredients in).
5. Add shredded squash and spinach to sausage mixture and cook until tender (about 3–5 minutes).
6. Make wells in the mixture to nestle the eggs in. Crack the eggs over the wells and into them. (You may crack them in a bowl first before slipping them into the pan.)
7. Place in broiler and cook to desired doneness (about 5 minutes).

8. Let cool slightly and arrange avocado on top.
9. Garnish with chopped green onion and serve.

Nutrition (per serving)
Calories 637
Carbs 17.2 g
Fat 46.4 g
Protein 31.4 g
Sodium 801 mg

Eggs with Avocado and Spicy Tomatoes

Serves: 2
Preparation Time: 5 minutes
Cooking Time: 15 minutes

Ingredients
1 Tablespoon coconut oil
1 10-ounce candied tomatoes with chilies (like Ro-Tel)
1 ripe avocado, peeled and sliced thinly
4 eggs, at room temperature
Salt substitute or seasoning (like Spike), to taste
Black pepper, to taste
Red pepper flakes, to taste (optional)

Directions
1. Preheat oven to 400°F.
2. Spread oil over cast iron skillet and place over medium heat.
3. Add tomatoes and let simmer until liquid has evaporated (about 4–5 minutes).
4. Reduce heat to low.
5. Arrange avocado slices over tomato mixture.
6. Drop in eggs, spacing them apart, and season as desired.
7. Bake to desired doneness (about 10 minutes).
8. Sprinkle with red pepper flakes (if using) and serve.

Nutrition (per serving)
Calories 364
Carbs 10.3 g
Fat 29.9 g
Protein 14.3 g
Sodium 586 mg

Eggs, Spinach & Mushrooms in a Skillet

Serves: 2
Preparation Time: 5 minutes
Cooking Time: 17–20 minutes

Ingredients
1 Tablespoon olive oil
8 ounces mini bella mushrooms, chopped
2 Tablespoons water
5 cups spinach, firmly packed
4 eggs, at room temperature
2 Tablespoons butter
Salt and pepper, to taste

Directions
1. Heat the oil in the cast iron pan over medium heat.
2. Sauté the mushrooms until tender (about 8 minutes). Scoop out using a slotted spoon and transfer to a dish. Set aside.
3. Using the same skillet, add water and spinach. Cook until wilted (about 4 minutes).
4. Return the mushrooms to the skillet.
5. Season with salt and pepper.
6. Make four wells in the vegetables and add about ½ Tablespoon of butter to each well.
7. Carefully drop the eggs into the wells.
8. Season the eggs with salt and pepper.
9. Cook until eggs reach desired doneness (about 5 minutes).
10. Alternatively, you may place the whole skillet under a preheated broiler and let cook until done (2–3 minutes).

Nutrition (per serving)
Calories 169
Carbs 2.8 g
Fat 14.1 g
Protein 8.4 g
Sodium 547 mg

Huevos Rancheros

Serves: 4
Preparation Time: 15 minutes
Cooking Time: 15–20 minutes

Ingredients
1 Tablespoon olive oil, plus more for greasing
½ onion, chopped
2 cloves garlic, minced
2 tomatoes, diced, divided
2 cups cooked beans, rinsed
1 teaspoon ground cumin
1 teaspoon dried coriander
½ teaspoon chipotle powder
½ teaspoon smoked paprika
Salt and freshly ground black pepper, to taste
2 Tablespoons water
4–6 6-inch tortillas (enough to line cast iron pan)
4 eggs
½ cup crumbled feta or goat cheese (optional)
1 large avocado, sliced
2 Tablespoons fresh cilantro, chopped
1 lime, cut into wedges
Hot sauce, to taste

Directions
1. Preheat oven to 400°F.
2. Heat oil in a large pan over medium heat.
3. Add onion and sauté until tender (about 5 minutes).
4. Add garlic and sauté until fragrant (about 1–2 minutes).
5. Add beans, spices, salt, water and half of the tomatoes.
6. Reduce heat to medium low and let simmer, stirring occasionally.

7. Prepare cast iron skillet. Brush with oil and line with tortillas. The tortillas should come up the sides of the skillet.
8. Brush tortillas with more olive oil.
9. Spread bean mixture evenly over tortillas.
10. Make four wells in the beans and drop eggs in.
11. Season with salt and pepper to taste and sprinkle with cheese.
12. Bake until eggs are done (about 10 minutes).
13. Top with cilantro, remaining tomatoes and avocado.
14. Serve with lime wedges and hot sauce.

Nutrition (per serving)
Calories 530
Carbs 62.4 g
Fat 23.9 g
Protein 21.6 g
Sodium 1255 mg

Shakshuka (Eggs Poached in Spicy Sauce)

Serves: 6
Preparation Time: 10 minutes
Cooking Time: 20 minutes

Ingredients
2 Tablespoons coconut oil
1 medium onion, chopped
1 medium bell pepper, sliced
4 cloves garlic, peeled and minced
1 teaspoon sweet paprika
½ teaspoon cumin
¼ teaspoon red pepper flakes, or to taste
¼ teaspoon salt
Black pepper, to taste
1 28-ounce can tomato sauce
¼–⅓ cup feta cheese, crumbled
6 eggs, at room temperature
Parsley and mint leaves, chopped, for garnish

Directions
1. Heat the oil in a cast iron skillet over medium heat.
2. Add onion, bell pepper, garlic, spices, salt and pepper.
3. Sauté until vegetables are tender (about 10 minutes).
4. Add tomato sauce and let simmer until mixture thickens (about 10 minutes).
5. Stir in crumbled feta. Adjust flavor of sauce with more salt, pepper and spices, as desired.
6. Crack eggs over the sauce and drop them in, being careful not to break the yolks. (You may also crack them one at a time in a bowl first and then slip each into the sauce.)
7. Reduce heat and cover skillet.

8. Let cook until egg whites are set and yolks are done as desired (about 10 minutes).
9. Garnish with parsley and mint leaves.
10. Serve immediately with pita or any crusty bread.

Nutrition (per serving)
Calories 185
Carbs 12.9 g
Fat 11.2 g
Protein 9.4 g
Sodium 934 mg

Beef Recipes

Perfect Pan-Seared Steak

Serves: 4
Preparation Time: 5 minutes
Cooking Time: 5–7 minutes

Ingredients
1 1½-pound rib eye steak or sirloin steak, 1½ inches thick
Salt and pepper, to taste
2 teaspoons olive oil
3 Tablespoons butter
2 cloves garlic, peeled
Handful fresh parsley sprigs
Splash or red wine

Directions
1. Heat cast iron skillet over high heat to smoking.
2. Meanwhile, season top of steak liberally with salt and pepper.
3. Add oil to hot skillet and swirl.
4. Place the steak seasoned-side down in the skillet and let cook for 2 minutes. Season the top while cooking the other side.
5. Flip steak over with a pair of tongs and let cook another 2 minutes.
6. Add butter, garlic and parsley to the skillet, beside the steak.
7. Ladle the melted butter over the top of the steak continuously, to baste.
8. Keep flipping and basting at 30-second intervals. Continue until desired doneness is reached (about 5 minutes for medium rare and 7 minutes for medium well). If using a thermometer, internal temperature should be 140°F for medium rare and 155°F for medium well.

9. Turn off heat and baste the steak one last time. Cover loosely with foil and let sit for 5–10 minutes.
10. Transfer steak to a chopping board.
11. Heat skillet with drippings over medium heat. Add wine to deglaze, scraping brown bits from bottom.
12. Pour sauce over steak and slice.

Nutrition (per serving)
Calories 430
Carbs 1.2 g
Fat 22.3 g
Protein 51.9 g
Sodium 320 mg

Beef Tenderloin Steaks and Balsamic Green Beans

Serves: 4
Preparation Time: 5 minutes
Cooking Time: 25 minutes

Ingredients
2 teaspoons butter, divided
2 large yellow onions, sliced
3 garlic cloves, minced
½ cup beef broth
2 cups green beans, trimmed
2 Tablespoons balsamic vinegar
¼ teaspoon salt, divided
1 teaspoon coconut oil or cooking spray
4 4-ounce beef tenderloin steaks
¼ teaspoon freshly ground black pepper

Directions
1. Melt 1 teaspoon butter in a saucepan over medium high heat.
2. Add onions and sauté until translucent (about 5 minutes).
3. Add garlic and sauté until fragrant (about 1 minute).
4. Stir in broth and cook until reduced (about 4 minutes).
5. Add beans and stir until bright green in color (about 2 minutes).
6. Add balsamic vinegar, cover and cook until beans are crisp-tender (about 3 minutes).
7. Turn off heat and stir in remaining butter.
8. Sprinkle with ⅛ teaspoon salt.
9. Meanwhile, season steaks with remaining salt and pepper.
10. Heat cast iron skillet over medium high heat.

11. Swirl in oil or spray with cooking spray.
12. Cook steaks to desired doneness (about 3 minutes per side).
13. Turn off heat and let stand for 5 minutes.
14. Serve with bean mixture.

Nutrition (per serving)

Calories 244

Carbs 12.4 g

Fat 9.4 g

Protein 27.1 g

Sodium 285 mg

Steak with Chermoula

Serves: 6
Preparation Time: 5–10 minutes
Cooking Time: 8 minutes

Ingredients
Chermoula:
1 cup fresh parsley leaves
1 cup fresh cilantro leaves
1 Tablespoon paprika
3 Tablespoons beef broth
2 Tablespoons fresh lime juice
1 Tablespoon olive oil
1 teaspoon ground cumin
½ teaspoon ground coriander
¼ teaspoon salt
¼ teaspoon ground red pepper
4 garlic cloves, peeled

Steak:
1 1½-pound flank steak, trimmed
¼ teaspoon salt
¼ teaspoon freshly ground black pepper
Cooking spray or cooking oil for greasing

Directions
1. Prepare chermoula by adding ingredients to a blender or food processor. Pulse until a paste is formed. Set aside.
2. Season the steaks with salt and pepper.
3. Heat cast iron skillet over high heat.
4. Spray with cooking spray or swirl with oil.

5. Cook steak for 4 minutes on one side. Flip over and cook to desired doneness (about 4 minutes for medium rare). If using a thermometer, internal temperature should be 140°F for medium rare and 155°F for medium well.
6. Let rest for 5 minutes before slicing.
7. Serve with chermoula.

Nutrition (per serving)
Calories 195
Carbs 2.6 g
Fat 8.9 g
Protein 25.3 g
Sodium 284 mg

Cast-Iron Burgers

Serves: 4
Preparation Time: 20 minutes plus 30 minutes refrigeration
Cooking Time: 25–30 minutes

Ingredients
Patties:
1 pound ground sirloin
½ teaspoon salt

Horseradish spread:
1 Tablespoon canola mayonnaise
1 Tablespoon Dijon mustard
1 Tablespoon prepared horseradish
2 teaspoons ketchup

Relish:
2 applewood-smoked bacon slices, chopped
3 cups vertically sliced yellow onion
1 Tablespoon finely chopped chives
1 teaspoon Worcestershire sauce
¼ teaspoon freshly ground black pepper

Remaining ingredients:
Cooking spray
4 1½-ounce hamburger buns or Kaiser rolls
4 thick tomato slices
1 cup lettuce, shredded

Directions

1. Divide the ground sirloin into 4 portions. Pat them lightly together to make 4 ½-inch thick patties. Sprinkle with salt and refrigerate for 30 minutes.
2. Mix ingredients for horseradish spread together in a small bowl. Set aside.
3. To make relish, first place bacon in a cast iron skillet. Place on stovetop over low heat. Let bacon cook slowly until it begins to curl. Flip over several times until evenly crisp. Remove from skillet and drain over paper towels, to be chopped after draining. Cook the onions in the same skillet, using the bacon drippings, until browned (about 15 minutes). Transfer to a bowl along with other relish ingredients and chopped bacon. Set aside.
4. To cook patties, heat a clean cast iron skillet over medium high heat. Spray or grease with cooking oil. Add the patties and cook to desired doneness (about 2–3 minutes on each side).
5. To assemble burger, spread horseradish sauce over insides of a hamburger bun. Add a patty and top with relish, a slice of tomato and shredded cabbage. Repeat for the rest of the buns.

Nutrition (per serving)
Calories 351
Carbs 32.7 g
Fat 12 g
Protein 29.2 g
Sodium 788 mg

Fajitas with Chimichurri

Serves: 6
Preparation Time: 15 minutes plus 1 hour marinating time
Cooking Time: 15 minutes

Ingredients
1½ pounds flank steak, cut into 3 pieces
1 Tablespoon olive oil
1 red bell pepper, seeded and sliced
1 yellow pepper, seeded and sliced
1 poblano pepper, seeded and sliced
6–8 flour tortillas, warmed
Queso fresco or cotija cheese, crumbled
Guacamole or sliced avocado, for serving

Steak marinade
3 Tablespoons olive oil
1 teaspoon chili powder
1 teaspoon smoked paprika
½ teaspoon cumin
Zest and juice of 2 limes
Salt and pepper, to taste

Chimichurri
1 cup fresh cilantro, chopped finely
1 cup fresh parsley, chopped finely
1–2 jalapenos or Serrano chilies, seeded and chopped
4 cloves garlic, minced
½ cup olive oil
2 Tablespoons red wine vinegar
Salt, to taste

Cucumber Salsa
1 cucumber, diced
1 mango, peeled and diced
Juice of 2 limes
⅓ cup fresh cilantro, chopped
1–2 jalapenos, seeded and chopped
Salt, to taste

Directions
1. Combine the marinade ingredients in a shallow container or large Ziploc bag. Marinate the steak, refrigerated, for 1 hour to overnight.
2. For chimichurri sauce, mix the ingredients well in a bowl. Cover and refrigerate.
3. For the cucumber salsa, toss ingredients together, cover and refrigerate.
4. To prepare steak fajitas, heat a large cast iron skillet over medium-high heat. Add olive oil, peppers, salt and pepper. Stir-fry until fragrant and tender (about 4–5 minutes). Using a slotted spoon, remove the pepper mixture from the skillet. Reheat the skillet and sear the steak on one side (about 3 minutes). Flip over and cook until the steak reaches your desired doneness (about 4–5 minutes). Remove from the heat and let rest for 5 minutes. Slice, against the grain, into strips.
5. To assemble, fill a tortilla with steak and peppers, drizzle with chimichurri sauce, and top with salsa and cheese.

Nutrition (per serving)
Calories 407
Carbs 19.2 g
Fat 21.5 g
Protein 35.5 g
Sodium 122 mg

Moroccan Steak with Roasted Pepper Couscous

Serves: 4
Preparation Time: 5 minutes
Cooking Time: 20 minutes

Ingredients
2 medium bell peppers
1 pound skirt steak or sirloin steak, about 1 inch thick, trimmed
1 Tablespoon extra-virgin olive oil
Lemon wedges, for garnish

Couscous Mixture
1 teaspoon spice mix (see below)
1 teaspoon extra-virgin olive oil
Juice of 1 lemon
Zest of ½ lemon
¾ cup water
⅔ cup whole-wheat couscous
2 Tablespoons green olives, chopped

Spice Mix
1 teaspoon ground cumin
1 teaspoon ground coriander
¾ teaspoon salt
½ teaspoon ground turmeric
½ teaspoon ground cinnamon
½ teaspoon freshly ground pepper

Directions

1. Preheat broiler.
2. Roast bell peppers under broiler until tender, with surface charred (about 10–15 minutes). Flip over occasionally for even roasting. Let cool and then chop. Set aside (to be mixed with couscous later).
3. Meanwhile, combine ingredients for spice mix. Separate 1 teaspoon for couscous and rub the rest over the steak. Let stand.
4. Prepare couscous. In a saucepan, take 1 teaspoon of the spice mix and combine with lemon zest and juice. Add water and bring to a boil. Stir in couscous and remove from heat. Cover and let cool slightly. Stir in olives and peppers. Set aside.
5. Heat cast iron skillet over medium high heat. Swirl in oil and heat until oil shimmers. Cook the steak to desired doneness (about 2–3 minutes on each side for medium rare; 140°F internal temperature for medium rare and 155°F for medium well). Let stand for 5 minutes before slicing.
6. Serve immediately with couscous and lemon wedges.

Nutrition (per serving)

Calories 454
Carbs 36 g
Fat 18 g
Protein 36 g
Sodium 663 mg

Strip Steaks with Smoky Cilantro Sauce & Roasted Vegetables

Serves: 4
Preparation Time: 10 minutes
Cooking Time: 20 minutes

Ingredients
2 8-ounce strip steaks, trimmed and halved
1 Tablespoon extra virgin olive oil
½ teaspoon salt
½ teaspoon black pepper

Vegetables:
2 Tablespoons extra virgin olive oil
1 pound Brussels sprouts, trimmed and quartered
1 large sweet potato, peeled and cubed
¼ teaspoon salt
¼ teaspoon ground pepper

Sauce:
2 Tablespoons extra virgin olive oil
½ teaspoon brown sugar
1 cup packed fresh cilantro
1 small fresh red chili, seeded and chopped
1 large clove garlic, finely grated
1 Tablespoon tomato paste
2 teaspoons red-wine vinegar
1 teaspoon smoked paprika
½ teaspoon ground cumin

Directions

1. Preheat oven to 450°F.
2. Place sauce ingredients in a blender or food processor and pulse to make into a puree. Set aside.
3. To prepare vegetables, heat cast iron pan over high heat. Swirl in oil and reduce heat to medium. Add vegetables and season with salt and pepper. Sauté until vegetables are half-cooked (about 10 minutes). Use a slotted spoon to transfer to a plate. Set aside.
4. Add the oil for the steaks to the skillet to heat. Season the steaks and cook to brown (1 minute on both sides).
5. Add the vegetables to the skillet, with the steaks.
6. Pour about half of the sauce over the steaks.
7. Place in oven and bake to desired doneness (about 8–10 minutes; 140°F internal temperature for medium rare and 155°F for medium well).
8. Remove from heat.
9. Stir remaining sauce into vegetables.
10. Serve.

Nutrition (per serving)

Calories 399
Carbs 22 g
Fat 23 g
Protein 27 g
Sodium 559 mg

Steak with Glazed Carrots & Turnips

Serves: 4
Preparation Time: 5 minutes
Cooking Time: 20–25 minutes

Ingredients
2 Tablespoons extra-virgin olive oil, divided
1 Tablespoon butter
1 pound small carrots, halved lengthwise
3 medium turnips, peeled and cut into thick matchsticks
¾ teaspoon salt, divided
¾ teaspoon ground pepper, divided
1 pound sirloin steak, about 1 inch thick, trimmed and halved crosswise
1 teaspoon minced fresh rosemary or ½ teaspoon dried rosemary
2 Tablespoons brown sugar
1 Tablespoon red-wine vinegar

Directions
1. Preheat oven to 450°F.
2. Season steak pieces with ½ teaspoon each of salt and pepper plus the rosemary. Set aside.
3. Heat cast iron skillet over medium high heat.
4. Add 1 Tablespoon oil plus butter.
5. Add carrots and turnips.
6. Sprinkle with ¼ teaspoon each of salt and pepper.
7. Sauté until browned and beginning to soften (about 10 minutes).
8. Use a slotted spoon to transfer veggies to a plate.
9. Add the remaining oil to the skillet and heat to almost smoking.
10. Sear the steak (2 minutes on both sides).
11. Return the veggies to the skillet with the steak.

43

12. Stir brown sugar into the veggies.
13. Bake until steak reaches desired doneness (about 8 minutes; 140°F internal temperature for medium rare and 155°F for medium well).
14. Transfer steak to a chopping board and let rest for 5 minutes before slicing.
15. Stir vinegar into vegetables.
16. Slice steak and serve with vegetables.

Nutrition (per serving)
Calories 328
Carbs 25 g
Fat 15 g
Protein 24 g
Sodium 639 mg

Spiced Sirloin Steak

Serves: 4
Preparation Time: 10 minutes
Cooking Time: 14 minutes

Ingredients
Oil for greasing, or cooking spray
1 Tablespoon brown sugar
½ teaspoon salt
½ teaspoon ground cumin
½ teaspoon ground coriander seeds
¼ teaspoon ground red pepper
1 pound boneless sirloin steak (about 1¼ inches thick), trimmed

Directions
1. Preheat oven to 450°F.
2. Grease cast iron skillet.
3. Place pan in oven for 5 minutes.
4. Meanwhile, combine brown sugar, salt and spices and rub evenly over steak.
5. Place steak in preheated pan.
6. Bake to desired doneness (about 7 minutes on each side).
7. Let stand for 3–5 minutes before slicing.

Nutrition (per serving)
Calories 198
Carbs 3.7 g
Fat 8.6 g
Protein 25.1 g
Sodium 350 mg

Pork Recipes

Braised Cabbage and Mushrooms with Pancetta

Serves: 4
Preparation Time: 5 minutes
Cooking Time: 30 minutes

Ingredients
3 teaspoons butter, divided
1–2 strips pancetta or bacon, chopped
2 medium leeks, washed, drained and sliced thinly
¼ teaspoon salt
¼ teaspoon freshly ground pepper
½ cup chicken broth or water
6 cups shredded cabbage
8 ounces sliced mushrooms

Directions
1. Heat butter in cast iron pan over low heat.
2. Cook pancetta until browned (about 5 minutes). Use a slotted spoon to transfer to a plate lined with paper towels. Set aside.
3. To the same skillet, add the remaining butter, sliced leeks, broth, salt and pepper.
4. Bring to a boil, reduce heat and cover. Let simmer until leeks are tender (about 5 minutes).
5. Add cabbage, cover, and continue simmering until cabbage is wilted and turning translucent (about 15 minutes). Add more broth or water by the tablespoonful if needed to prevent mixture from drying out.
6. Add mushrooms, cover, and simmer until all veggies are tender (about 5 minutes).
7. Sprinkle with pancetta and serve.

Nutrition (per serving)
Calories 148
Carbs 21 g
Fat 6 g
Protein 7 g
Sodium 375 mg

Spiced Pork with Apples

Serves: 4
Preparation Time: 5 minutes
Cooking Time: 15 minutes

Ingredients
Cooking spray or oil for greasing
1 pound pork tenderloin, trimmed and cut crosswise into 12 or more pieces
2 Tablespoons butter
2 cups apple, sliced
⅓ cup shallots or red onion, thinly sliced
⅛ teaspoon salt
¼ cup apple cider
1 teaspoon fresh thyme leaves

Spice Mix:
⅓ teaspoon salt
¼ teaspoon freshly ground black pepper
¼ teaspoon ground coriander
⅛ teaspoon ground cinnamon
⅛ teaspoon ground nutmeg

Directions
1. Combine ingredients for spice mix and rub over pork.
2. Heat cast iron pan over medium high heat. Spray or grease with oil and cook pork to desired doneness (about 3 minutes on each side; at least 145°F internal temperature). Use a slotted spoon to transfer to a plate and let rest.
3. In the same skillet, swirl in the butter to melt. Add the apple, shallots and salt. Sauté until browned (about 5 minutes). Add apple cider and cook until tender-crisp.
4. Add sautéed apples to pork and serve.

Nutrition (per serving)
Calories 234
Carbs 12.3 g
Fat 9.7 g
Protein 24.4 g
Sodium 394 mg

Pork with Mushrooms and Sweet Potato

Serves: 4
Preparation Time: 10 minutes
Cooking Time: 1 hour 30 minutes

Ingredients
1 pound pork shoulder, boneless, trimmed
½ teaspoon kosher salt
½ teaspoon black pepper
Cooking spray
3½ cups chicken broth
6 garlic cloves, crushed
1 Tablespoon olive oil
4 cups sweet potato, peeled and diced
1 cup onion, chopped
¼ teaspoon red pepper flakes
8 ounces cremini mushrooms, quartered
3 Tablespoons green onions, sliced

Directions
1. Season pork with salt and pepper.
2. Heat cast iron skillet over medium high heat and coat with cooking spray or oil.
3. Sear pork, flipping over occasionally, until evenly browned (about 10 minutes).
4. Add broth and garlic and bring to a boil.
5. Cover and reduce heat. Let simmer until pork is tender enough to shred with a fork (about 45 minutes).
6. Reserving cooking liquid (with the garlic), use a slotted spoon to transfer the pork to a chopping board.
7. Let the pork rest (about 3–5 minutes) and then shred. Set aside.
8. Heat a clean cast iron skillet over medium high heat.

9. Swirl in olive oil and sauté sweet potato and onion until lightly browned (about 5–8 minutes).
10. Add red pepper flakes and mushroom and sauté until fragrant and moisture from mushrooms is released (about 3 minutes).
11. Add reserved liquid and bring to a boil.
12. Reduce heat to medium and let simmer uncovered, stirring occasionally, until liquid is reduced or until almost dry (about 20 minutes).
13. Stir in pork and cook to heat through (about 1 minute).
14. Sprinkle with green onion and serve.

Nutrition (per serving)
Calories 340
Carbs 29 g
Fat 11.8 g
Protein 28.3 g
Sodium 732 mg

Pork Chops Provençal with Potatoes

Serves: 4
Preparation Time: 5 minutes
Cooking Time: 17–20 minutes

Ingredients
2 medium potatoes (starchy, like Yukon gold or Idaho), diced
3 Tablespoons olive oil, divided
Salt and pepper, to taste
4 pork loin chops, boneless and trimmed, about ¾ inch thick
¼ cup pitted Kalamata olives, chopped
4 teaspoons capers, drained
3 cloves garlic, peeled and smashed
3 sprigs thyme
1 cup cherry tomatoes, halved
½ cup white wine
½ cup chicken broth
Fresh parsley leaves, roughly chopped, for garnish

Directions
1. Season pork loin chops with salt and pepper.
2. Heat 2 Tablespoons oil in cast iron skillet until almost smoking.
3. Add diced potatoes (if soaked in water, drain and dry with paper towels first).
4. Sauté until browned at edges (about 5 minutes).
5. Push potatoes to side of skillet to make space for pork.
6. Cook pork until browned (about 3 minutes on each side), while stirring potatoes.
7. Push pork and potatoes further to sides to make way for other ingredients.
8. Add remaining oil and reduce heat.
9. Sauté olives, capers, garlic and thyme until fragrant (about 1 minute).

53

10. Add tomatoes and wine. Turn heat up to medium.
11. Cook until sauce is reduced to half (about 2 minutes).
12. Add broth, making sure pork and potatoes are well-moistened.
13. Cook until pork is done (about 3 minutes, with internal temperature of 145°F).
14. Transfer pork to serving dish.
15. Adjust consistency of sauce, as needed, by adding water if dry or cooking longer to reduce. Add more salt and pepper, as needed.
16. Fish out thyme sprigs and stir in parsley.
17. Spoon sauce over pork and serve.

Nutrition (per serving)
Calories 283
Carbs 20 g
Fat 9.1 g
Protein 23.5 g
Sodium 944 mg

Paella a la Cubana

Serves: 10
Preparation Time: 10 minutes
Cooking Time: 55–60 minutes

Ingredients
1 Tablespoon extra-virgin olive oil
1½ pounds boneless pork chops, trimmed, cut into cubes
2 Tablespoons garlic, chopped
2 cups onion, chopped
2 cups Arborio rice
2 14-ounce cans reduced-sodium chicken broth
1 cup tomatoes, diced
2 Tablespoons capers, rinsed
¼ teaspoon saffron threads
16 large raw shrimp, peeled and deveined (optional)
2 cups frozen artichoke hearts, thawed
½ cup roasted red peppers, cut into strips

Spice paste:
¼ cup paprika
¼ cup lime juice
2 Tablespoons extra-virgin olive oil
2 Tablespoons rum
2 teaspoons garlic, minced
2 teaspoons fresh oregano, chopped
1 teaspoon kosher salt
1 teaspoon freshly ground pepper
½ teaspoon ground cumin

Directions

1. Whisk together ingredients for spice paste in a bowl.
2. Add pork and coat well with paste.
3. Heat oil in cast iron skillet over medium high heat.
4. Transfer the pork, reserving remaining spice paste, to skillet.
5. Cook until pork begins to change color and spices are fragrant (about 3 minutes).
6. Transfer pork to a plate and set aside.
7. Preheat oven to 350°F.
8. To the same skillet, add garlic and onion. Sauté until tender (about 5 minutes).
9. Add rice, stirring constantly to coat with garlic mixture.
10. Add broth, tomatoes, capers and saffron.
11. Scrape in remaining spice paste.
12. Stir and bring to a boil.
13. Reduce heat and let simmer, stirring occasionally, for 15 minutes.
14. Stir in shrimp and artichokes and transfer to oven.
15. Place a lid over skillet or cover with foil and bake for 20 minutes.
16. Stir in pork and sprinkle with pepper strips.
17. Cover and continue baking until shrimps are done (pink and opaque) and rice is tender (about 10–15 minutes).

Nutrition (per serving)

Calories 294
Carbs 39 g
Fat 8 g
Protein 16 g
Sodium 398 mg

Pan Grilled Pork Chops

Serves: 4
Preparation Time: 5 minutes plus 30 minutes waiting time
Cooking Time: 15–20 minutes

Ingredients
4 pork chops, about ½–1 inch thick
1 teaspoon dried thyme
1 teaspoon salt
½ teaspoon fresh ground pepper
1–2 Tablespoons cooking oil
¼ cup red or white wine, broth or water
1–2 Tablespoons butter

Directions
1. Season pork chops with thyme, salt and pepper.
2. Let stand for 30 minutes.
3. Heat oil in cast iron skillet over medium high heat.
4. Reduce heat to medium and place pork chops into skillet.
5. Cook until browned (about 4 minutes on each side).
6. Place lid on skillet and turn off heat.
7. Let pork chops cook in residual heat (about 8–10 minutes).
8. Transfer pork chops to serving dish.
9. Reheat skillet over medium heat and add wine to deglaze.
10. Scrape bits and let liquid reduce.
11. Stir in butter.
12. Pour sauce over pork chops and serve.

Nutrition (per serving)
Calories 427
Carbs 0.6 g
Fat 27.2g
Protein 41.4 g
Sodium 732 mg

Pork Chops with Apples and Onions

Serves: 6
Preparation Time: 5 minutes
Cooking Time: 33–35 minutes

Ingredients
6 pork chops, bone-in, ¾ inch thick, trimmed
Salt and pepper, to taste
1 Tablespoon olive oil
2 Tablespoons unsalted butter
1 large onion, sliced
3 apples, cored and sliced
1 cup white wine or chicken broth

Directions
1. Season pork chops liberally with salt and pepper.
2. Heat cast iron skillet over high heat and swirl in olive oil.
3. Place pork chops in skillet and let brown thoroughly on one side before flipping over (about 10 minutes total cooking time). Transfer to a plate.
4. Melt butter in the same skillet.
5. Sauté onion and apple slices until onions begin to caramelize (about 8 minutes).
6. Stir in wine or broth and return pork chops to skillet.
7. Simmer until pork is tender (about 15 minutes).
8. Transfer pork chops to serving plate.
9. If needed, turn heat up to high to reduce and thicken apple-onion mixture.
10. Top pork chops with apple-onion mixture and serve.

Nutrition (per serving)
Calories 324
Carbs 10.1 g
Fat 19.5 g
Protein 20.3 g
Sodium 238 mg

Garlic Roasted Pork Chops

Serves: 4
Preparation Time: 5 minutes
Cooking Time: 7 minutes

Ingredients
4 pork chops, boneless, center-cut
1 Tablespoon olive oil
1 teaspoon sea salt
½ teaspoon ground black pepper
6–8 cloves garlic, peeled

Directions
1. Preheat oven to 400°F.
2. Season pork chops with salt and pepper.
3. Heat cast iron skillet over high heat and swirl in olive oil.
4. Sear pork chops on one side until well-browned (about 3 minutes).
5. Flip pork chops over and toss in garlic.
6. Place in oven and let roast for 2 minutes.
7. Flip chops and garlic over and bake until cooked through (about 2 minutes or to internal temperature of 145°F).
8. Transfer to serving dish, along with roasted garlic, and let rest for 5 minutes.
9. Serve.

Nutrition (per serving)
Calories 378
Carbs 2.3 g
Fat 21.4 g
Protein 41.6 g
Sodium 693 mg

Pork Medallions in Mushroom Gravy

Serves: 2–4
Preparation Time: 10 minutes
Cooking Time: 15 minutes

Ingredients
1½ pounds pork tenderloin
Salt and pepper, to taste
2–3 Tablespoons ghee or coconut oil
8 ounces baby bella mushrooms, sliced
1 cup chicken stock
1 Tablespoon fresh sage, chopped finely
1 teaspoon fresh thyme, chopped finely
1 Tablespoon tapioca starch (or 1½ teaspoons cornstarch)
1 Tablespoon water

Directions
1. Season the pork liberally with salt and pepper.
2. Slice into medallions of similar thickness (about 8–9 pieces).
3. Heat cast iron pan over medium high heat and swirl in ghee or oil.
4. Cook medallions until golden brown (about 4 minutes on each side).
5. Transfer to a plate and set aside.
6. Using the same skillet, sauté mushrooms until golden brown (about 5 minutes). You may need to add more oil.
7. Stir in chicken stock and herbs.
8. Pour in the starch mixed with water.
9. Bring mixture to a boil and cook, while stirring, until thickened (about 1 minute).
10. Return the medallions to the skillet with its juices.
11. Remove from heat but let the medallions soak in the sauce for about 5 minutes before serving.

Nutrition (per serving)
Calories 284
Carbs 5 g
Fat 10.1 g
Protein 34.1 g
Sodium 565 mg

Chicken Recipes

Middle Eastern Chicken with Chickpeas

Serves: 4
Preparation Time: 10 minutes
Cooking Time: 15–20 minutes

Ingredients
1 pound boneless, skinless chicken breasts, trimmed, cut into bite size pieces
¼ teaspoon salt
1 Tablespoon extra-virgin olive oil
1 large yellow onion, chopped
1 14-ounce can diced tomatoes
1 15-ounce can chickpeas, rinsed and drained
Parsley, chopped, for garnish

Seasoning mix:
4 cloves garlic, minced
½ teaspoon salt
¼ cup lemon juice
1 teaspoon ground cumin
1 teaspoon paprika
½ teaspoon ground pepper

Directions
1. Prepare the seasoning mix. First mash the garlic well with salt and then mix in a large bowl with the other seasoning ingredients.
2. Add chicken to the seasoning mix and toss to coat. Let sit briefly.
3. Heat the cast iron skillet over medium high heat and swirl in the oil.
4. Add onion and sauté until browned (about 5–8 minutes).
5. Transfer chicken, reserving the seasoning, to the skillet.

6. Sauté chicken until no longer pink on the outside (about 4 minutes).
7. Add reserved seasoning with the tomatoes and drained chickpeas.
8. Sprinkle with remaining salt.
9. Reduce heat and let simmer, with occasional stirring, until chicken is thoroughly cooked (about 5–10 minutes).
10. Sprinkle with parsley and serve.

Nutrition (per serving)

Calories 267
Carbs 21 g
Fat 8 g
Protein 28 g
Sodium 613 mg

Greek-Style One Pan Chicken and Rice

Serves: 6
Preparation Time: 5 minutes plus 1 hour marinating time
Cooking Time: 55–60 minutes

Ingredients
6 chicken thighs
2 Tablespoons olive oil, divided
1 Tablespoon fresh oregano, chopped
1 yellow onion, diced
1 cup basmati rice
2 cups chicken broth
¼ cup water
½ cup cherry tomatoes
¼ cup pitted Kalamata olives
½–1 lemon, sliced thinly
Freshly ground black pepper, to taste
Chopped fresh parsley, for garnish

Marinade:
¼ cup lemon juice
Zest of 1 lemon
2 Tablespoons fresh oregano, chopped
4 cloves garlic, diced
1 teaspoon salt

Directions
1. Combine marinade ingredients in a shallow container or Ziploc bag.
2. Add the chicken, cover or seal, and let marinate for at least 1 hour to overnight.
3. Preheat oven to 350°F.
4. Heat cast iron skillet over medium high heat and swirl in a Tablespoon of oil.

5. Carefully remove the chicken from the marinade (reserving the marinade) and lay skin-side down in the skillet.
6. Cook until skin is browned (about 3–5 minutes on each side).
7. Transfer chicken to a plate and set aside.
8. Remove any bits of chicken from the skillet and wipe clean with paper towels. (Do this carefully, as skillet is hot!)
9. Swirl in remaining oil and onion. Cook until onion pieces begin to brown at the edges (about 5 minutes).
10. Stir in the reserved marinade, rice, broth, water, tomatoes, and olives.
11. Bring to a boil.
12. Reduce heat and let simmer briefly (30 seconds).
13. Place chicken on top and cover with fitted lid or aluminum foil.
14. Bake for 30 minutes.
15. Remove lid and place lemon slices on top.
16. Bake until chicken is browned and liquid has evaporated (about 10 minutes).
17. Remove from oven and let rest for 5–10 minutes.
18. Fluff rice with a fork.
19. Sprinkle with freshly ground black pepper and chopped parsley.
20. Serve.

Nutrition (per serving)
Calories 300
Carbs 29.4 g
Fat 10.4 g
Protein 21 g
Sodium 745 mg

Harvest Chicken with Sweet Potatoes, Brussels Sprouts and Apples

Serves: 4
Preparation Time: 5 minutes
Cooking Time: 30–35 minutes

Ingredients
1 Tablespoon olive oil
1 pound boneless, skinless chicken breasts, diced
1 teaspoon salt, divided
½ teaspoon black pepper
4 slices thick-cut bacon, chopped
3 cups Brussels sprouts, trimmed and quartered
1 medium sweet potato, peeled and diced
1 medium onion, chopped
2 Granny Smith apples, peeled, cored and cubed
4 cloves garlic, minced
2 teaspoons chopped fresh thyme
1 teaspoon ground cinnamon
1 cup reduced-sodium chicken broth, divided

Directions
1. Season chicken with ½ teaspoon salt and pepper.
2. Heat the oil in a cast iron skillet, over medium high heat, until shimmering hot.
3. Add chicken and cook until browned (about 5 minutes).
4. Drain chicken over paper towels and set aside.
5. Reduce heat to medium low and, using the same skillet, cook bacon until brown and crisp (about 8 minutes).
6. Reserving rendered fat, remove bacon and drain over paper towels.
7. Drain off any excess oil or fat from skillet, leaving about 1½ Tablespoons.

8. Turn heat up to medium high and add Brussels sprouts, sweet potato, onion, and remaining salt.
9. Sauté until onions are translucent and vegetables are crisp-tender (about 10 minutes).
10. Stir in apples, garlic, thyme, and cinnamon; cook until fragrant (about 1 minute).
11. Add ½ cup of broth and bring to a boil.
12. Boil until liquid has evaporated (about 2 minutes).
13. Add remaining broth and the drained chicken.
14. Let cook through (about 2 minutes).
15. Remove from heat and stir in bacon.
16. Serve.

Nutrition (per serving)
Calories 319
Carbs 26 g
Fat 11 g
Protein 32 g
Sodium 708 mg

Chicken and Vegetable Roast with Dijon Au Jus

Serves: 4
Preparation Time: 35 minutes
Cooking Time: 45–60 minutes

Ingredients

16 fingerling or yellow new potatoes, scrubbed
3 large carrots, cut into 1-inch chunks, divided
Salt and pepper, to taste
16 Brussels sprouts, halved
4 Tablespoons extra-virgin olive oil, divided
1 whole 4-pound chicken, cut into 8 serving pieces, backbone reserved
1 cup dry white wine
1 whole onion, halved
1 stalk celery, roughly chopped
3–4 sprigs fresh sage
2 bay leaves
2 cups low-sodium chicken stock
1 medium shallot, sliced thinly
2 Tablespoons fresh parsley leaves, minced
2 Tablespoons unsalted butter
1 Tablespoon Dijon mustard
Juice of 1 lemon
2 teaspoons fish sauce

Directions

1. Place potatoes and 2 cups carrot chunks in a saucepan and cover with water. Add about ½ teaspoon of salt and bring to a boil. Let simmer until tender (about 10 minutes). Drain and transfer to a large bowl. Set aside empty saucepan for later.

2. Add Brussels sprouts to carrots and potatoes. Season with salt and pepper. Add 2 Tablespoons olive oil and toss to coat. Set aside.
3. To the saucepan, add the chicken backbone, 1 cup carrots, onion, celery, sage and bay leaves. Set aside.
4. Preheat oven to 450°F.
5. Pat chicken pieces dry with paper towels and season with salt and pepper.
6. Heat 1 Tablespoon oil in cast iron skillet over high heat.
7. When oil just begins to smoke, add chicken, skin-side down. Reduce heat so as not to burn the oil.
8. Cook on skin-side until golden brown (about 8 minutes), then flip over and brown the other side (about 3 minutes).
9. Transfer chicken to a plate.
10. In the same skillet, pour in white wine. Scrape any brown bits.
11. Carefully transfer white wine from skillet to saucepan with chicken backbone and veggies.
12. Wipe skillet clean.
13. Transfer any juices collected from chicken pieces to saucepan with backbone and veggies.
14. Pour in chicken stock and bring mixture to a simmer.
15. Reduce heat to lowest setting, cover and let cook as chicken and other ingredients roast in the oven.
16. Reheat cast iron skillet with remaining oil.
17. When oil just begins to smoke, add potato-carrot-Brussels sprouts mixture and spread evenly.
18. Place chicken pieces, skin-side up, on veggies.
19. Place in center rack of oven and let roast until chicken pieces are done (about 20–45 minutes, with internal temperature of 150°F for breasts and 165°F for other pieces).
20. Transfer chicken pieces to serving plate.

21. Add shallot to veggies. Flipping occasionally, roast veggies until browned (about 10 minutes). Remove from oven.
22. Sprinkle roasted vegetables with parsley and arrange chicken on top.
23. Make the Dijon sauce. Go back to the simmering mixture in the saucepan and drain the broth into a bowl. Whisk in butter, mustard, lemon juice and fish sauce. Adjust flavor with salt and pepper, according to taste.
24. Serve the chicken and veggies with the sauce.

Nutrition (per serving)
Calories 240
Carbs 36.5 g
Fat 3.1 g
Protein 15.7 g
Sodium 580 mg

Honey-Lemon Chicken

Serves: 4
Preparation Time: 5 minutes
Cooking Time: 35–40 minutes

Ingredients
4 large chicken thighs
½ cup lemon juice
¼ cup olive oil
1 clove garlic, minced
1 teaspoon salt
½ teaspoon dried oregano
1 Tablespoon honey
Parsley, chopped, for garnish

Directions
1. Preheat broiler (about 450–500°F).
2. Place chicken, skin-side down, in cast iron pan.
3. Broil chicken for 30 minutes, flipping halfway through.
4. While broiling chicken, whisk together lemon juice, olive oil, garlic, salt and oregano.
5. Brush some of the sauce over the chicken and broil until chicken appears brown and crisp (about 3–5 minutes).
6. Transfer skillet to stovetop.
7. Transfer chicken to serving dish, leaving drippings in skillet.
8. Remove any chicken bits from the skillet and drain out any drippings in excess of a couple of Tablespoons.
9. Stir in remaining sauce and honey to the skillet.
10. Bring the mixture to a boil and pour over chicken.
11. Sprinkle with parsley and serve.

Nutrition (per serving)
Calories 393
Carbs 7 g
Fat 32.4 g
Protein 18.9 g
Sodium 674 mg

Chicken Cheesesteaks with Chipotle

Serves: 4
Preparation Time: 5 minutes
Cooking Time: 12–15 minutes

Ingredients
1–2 pieces (or to taste) chilies from canned chipotle chilies in adobo sauce, minced
1 Tablespoon adobo sauce
2 teaspoons olive oil, divided
12 ounces chicken cutlets, sliced thinly
1 cup onion, sliced thinly
1 cup red bell pepper, pitted and sliced
4 cloves garlic, minced
¼ teaspoon dried thyme or oregano
¼ teaspoon salt
1 cup shredded cheddar cheese
4 hotdog buns or flour tortillas
Lime wedges (optional)

Directions
1. Heat 1 teaspoon oil in cast iron skillet over medium high heat.
2. Sauté chicken until done (about 4–5 minutes). Remove from skillet and set aside.
3. Add remaining oil to the still-hot skillet.
4. Sauté onion, garlic, bell pepper and thyme/oregano until fragrant and tender (about 4 minutes).
5. Add minced chilies and adobo sauce and let heat through (about 30 seconds).
6. Stir in chicken and season with salt. Cook to heat through (about 1 minute). Remove from heat.
7. Add cheese to warm mixture and stir to melt.
8. Fill buns or tortillas and serve with lime wedges, if using.

Nutrition (per serving)
Calories 388
Carbs 35.2 g
Fat 13 g
Protein 32.8 g
Sodium 605 mg

Crispy Roast Chicken

Serves: 4
Preparation Time: 10 minutes
Cooking Time: 80 minutes

Ingredients
1 4-pound whole chicken, giblets removed
3–4 Tablespoons olive oil or softened butter, or to taste
1 Tablespoon salt
Freshly ground black pepper, to taste

Directions
1. Preheat oven to 375°F.
2. Pat chicken dry with paper towels, as thoroughly as possible.
3. Rub oil or butter all over chicken.
4. Season with salt and pepper, including the inside cavity.
5. Truss or tie chicken legs together with kitchen twine.
6. Heat cast iron skillet over medium high heat and, using a pair of tongs, sear chicken to brown as evenly as possible (about 3 minutes on each side).
7. Position chicken, breast-side up, in cast iron pan and place in oven.
8. Let roast until evenly browned and juices run clear (about 80 minutes, with internal temperature of 165°F at thickest part of thigh).
9. Remove from heat and transfer chicken to chopping board.
10. Tent with foil and let rest for 15 minutes before carving.

Nutrition (per serving)
Calories 585
Carbs 0 g
Fat 44 g
Protein 42 g
Sodium 560 mg

Chicken Garlic Pasta

Serves: 6
Preparation Time: 10 minutes
Cooking Time: 45 minutes

Ingredients
1 pound boneless chicken breast, cut into bite size pieces
3 Tablespoons olive oil, divided
1 Tablespoon butter
1 teaspoon Italian seasoning
Salt and pepper, to taste
½ cup onion chopped
2 cloves garlic, minced
2½ cups chicken broth
1 14½-ounce can diced tomatoes
2½ cups penne pasta, uncooked
Red pepper flakes, to taste
½ cup half and half
1 cup mozzarella cheese, shredded

Directions
1. Preheat cast iron skillet over medium high heat.
2. Add 1½ Tablespoons of olive oil.
3. Stir in butter to melt.
4. Add chicken pieces, Italian seasoning, salt and pepper, cooking until golden brown (about 15 minutes).
5. Transfer chicken to a plate and set aside.
6. To the same skillet, add remaining olive oil and onions.
7. Reduce heat and cook until onion is translucent (about 5 minutes).
8. Add garlic and cook until fragrant (about 1 minute).
9. Stir in chicken broth and diced tomatoes (undrained).
10. Add pasta, red pepper flakes and cooked chicken pieces.
11. Bring mixture to a boil.

12. Cover, reduce heat to low and simmer until pasta is tender (about 15 minutes).
13. Stir in half & half and mozzarella cheese.
14. Remove from heat.
15. Let stand about 10 minutes and serve.

Nutrition (per serving)
Calories 67
Carbs 2.6 g
Fat 5.1 g
Protein 2.8 g
Sodium 341 mg

Cilantro-Lime Chicken with Rice and Black Beans

Serves: 4
Preparation Time: 5 minutes
Cooking Time: 12–14 minutes

Ingredients
1¼ pounds chicken breasts, boneless, skinless, and diced
Salt and pepper, to taste
1 Tablespoon olive oil
1 medium red bell pepper, seeded and diced
3 cups cooked rice
1 15-ounce can black beans, drained and rinsed
1 cup corn kernels, precooked
¾ cup cilantro leaves, chopped
1 lime, cut into wedges

Sauce:
3 Tablespoons lime zest
⅓ cup lime juice
⅓ cup honey
2 Tablespoons olive oil
¼ teaspoon cayenne pepper, or to taste
½ teaspoon salt, or to taste
¼ teaspoon pepper, or to taste

Directions
1. Season chicken with salt and pepper. Let sit.
2. Whisk ingredients for sauce in a bowl and set aside.
3. Heat cast iron skillet over medium high heat and swirl in oil.
4. Sauté chicken until browned at the edges (about 5 minutes).

5. Add bell peppers and sauce.
6. Let boil, while constantly flipping chicken pieces, until reduced and chicken is cooked through (about 4 minutes).
7. Stir in the rest of the ingredients and reduce heat to low.
8. Use a shoveling motion to mix until heated through (about 3–5 minutes). Adjust flavor with seasonings, as needed.
9. Serve with lime wedges.

Nutrition (per serving)
Calories 667
Carbs 100 g
Fat 9 g
Protein 47.7 g
Sodium 810 mg

One-Pot Chicken with Honey-Mustard Sauce

Serves: 4
Preparation Time: 10 minutes
Cooking Time: 60 minutes

Ingredients
3 Tablespoons olive oil, divided
2 medium onions, finely diced
3–4 pieces medium potatoes, sliced thinly
Salt and pepper, to taste
3–4 large chicken breasts, skinless and boneless, cut into thick strips
A bunch of fresh rosemary

For the sauce
2 Tablespoons Dijon mustard
3 Tablespoons grainy mustard
Juice of 1 large lemon
1 Tablespoon olive oil
3 Tablespoons honey
2 cloves garlic, minced
Salt and pepper, to taste

Directions
1. Whisk ingredients for sauce together, adjusting saltiness or sweetness according to taste. Set aside.
2. Preheat oven to 400°F.
3. Add 2 Tablespoons oil and onions to cast iron skillet and heat over medium high heat.
4. Sauté onions until tender and browned at the edges (about 8–10 minutes).
5. Remove from heat.
6. Spread onion slices in a single layer over bottom of skillet and carefully lay potatoes on top, also in a single layer.

7. Season with salt and pepper and then drizzle with remaining olive oil.
8. Cover with foil and bake until potatoes are tender (about 15–20 minutes).
9. Remove from oven and arrange chicken slices on top.
10. Pour prepared sauce over chicken, coating well.
11. Place rosemary on top of chicken and re-cover.
12. Bake for 20 minutes.
13. Remove foil and transfer to top rack to broil at high heat.
14. Broil until browned (about 15 minutes).
15. Serve while hot.

Nutrition (per serving)
Calories 482
Carbs 44.5 g
Fat 14.4 g
Protein 35.1g
Sodium 448 mg

Chicken Fajitas

Serves: 4
Preparation Time: 10 minutes plus 1 hour marinating time
Cooking Time: 15 minutes

Ingredients
1½ pounds chicken breasts, skinless, boneless, sliced ½-inch thick
Salt, to taste
2 Tablespoons high-smoke-point oil like canola, safflower, or avocado oil, divided
1 large onion, sliced vertically
3 bell peppers (assorted colors), sliced into thin strips
8–12 flour tortillas, warmed
Optional toppings: Salsa, guacamole, rice, avocado slices, sour cream, shredded lettuce or slaw

Marinade:
2 Tablespoons lime juice
3 Tablespoons olive oil
1 garlic clove, minced
½ teaspoon salt
½ teaspoon ground cumin
½ teaspoon chili powder
½ jalapeno, seeded and minced
¼ cup chopped cilantro

Directions
1. Combine marinade ingredients and place in shallow container or Ziploc bag with chicken. Let marinate, refrigerated, for 1–8 hours.
2. Drain out marinade and wipe chicken strips dry.
3. Sprinkle with salt.

4. Heat cast iron skillet over high heat for about 2 minutes and then swirl in 1 Tablespoon oil.
5. Sear chicken well on one side before flipping over to sear the other side (about 3 minutes on each side).
6. While keeping skillet warm, place seared chicken on a sheet of foil and cover loosely. Let rest while preparing other ingredients (about 5 minutes).
7. Add remaining oil to skillet and turn heat up to high.
8. Stir in onions and peppers, coating well with oil and any browned bits from chicken.
9. Sear vegetables until browned at edges (about 2 minutes per side). Remove from heat.
10. Slice the chicken into strips.
11. While warm, fill tortillas with chicken and pepper mixture along with toppings of choice.

Nutrition (per serving)
Calories 330
Carbs 23 g
Fat 11 g
Protein 21 g
Sodium 500 mg

Sesame Chicken

Serves: 2–4
Preparation Time: 5 minutes
Cooking Time: 25–30 minutes

Ingredients
2 pounds chicken breasts, boneless, skinless, cubed
½ teaspoon salt
½ teaspoon pepper
3 Tablespoons flour
1 Tablespoon olive oil
1 Tablespoon toasted sesame oil
2 Tablespoons toasted sesame seeds

Stock mixture:
½ cup low-sodium chicken stock
1 Tablespoon brown sugar
1 Tablespoon toasted sesame oil
2 garlic cloves, minced
1 Tablespoon low-sodium soy sauce
1 Tablespoon white vinegar

Directions
1. Preheat oven to 400°F.
2. In a bowl, whisk stock mixture ingredients together. Set aside.
3. Season chicken cubes with salt and pepper.
4. Heat cast iron skillet over medium high heat.
5. Swirl in olive and sesame oils.
6. Brown the chicken in the oil, flipping only once (about 2–3 minutes per side).
7. Add stock mixture and toss chicken to coat.
8. Place in oven and bake until golden and glazed (about 20 minutes).

9. Remove from oven and sprinkle with sesame seeds.
10. Goes well with veggies and rice.

Nutrition (per serving)
Calories 438
Carbs 9.9 g
Fat 20.8 g
Protein 52.5 g
Sodium 416 mg

Maple-Spice Turkey Breast

Serves: 8
Preparation Time: 10 minutes plus 20 minutes marinating time
Cooking Time: 30 minutes

Ingredients
2 skinless, boneless turkey breast halves (about 1½ pounds per piece)
Cooking spray

Marinade:
3 Tablespoons maple syrup
1 Tablespoon olive oil
2 teaspoons ground cumin
1 teaspoon kosher salt
1 teaspoon dried oregano
1 teaspoon smoked paprika
½ teaspoon ground coriander
½ teaspoon freshly ground black pepper

Sauce:
 2 teaspoons olive oil
⅔ cup onion, chopped
1 teaspoon garlic, minced
1¼ cups unsalted chicken stock
1 Tablespoon flour
¼ teaspoon kosher salt
¼ teaspoon freshly ground black pepper

Directions
1. Preheat oven to 450°F.
2. Combine marinade ingredients.
3. Marinate turkey breasts for 20 minutes at room temperature.

85

4. Remove turkey breasts and discard marinade.
5. Place in cast iron pan and bake until internal temperature reaches 155°F (about 25 minutes).
6. Transfer to chopping board, tent loosely with aluminum foil, and let rest for 10 minutes.
7. While turkey breast is resting, prepare sauce. Heat oil in a saucepan or frying pan over medium high heat. Sauté onion and garlic until tender (about 4 minutes). Mix flour with stock in a bowl and whisk into onion mixture. Bring to a boil, stirring continuously, until mixture begins to thicken (about 2 minutes). Remove from heat and stir in salt and pepper.
8. Slice rested turkey breast into 16 slices, against the grain.
9. Serve with sauce.

Nutrition (per serving)
Calories 205
Carbs 7.9 g
Fat 3.9 g
Protein 36.6 g
Sodium 385 mg

Chicken Roast over Fennel, Parsnips, and Scallions

Serves: 14
Preparation Time: 10 minutes
Cooking Time: 40–45 minutes

Ingredients
3 Tablespoons olive oil, divided
1 4-pound whole chicken
Salt and pepper, to taste
1 fennel bulb, sliced lengthwise ½ inch thick
2 large parsnips, peeled, sliced ½ inch thick on the diagonal
1 bunch scallions
3 wide strips lemon zest
Lemon wedges

Directions
1. Preheat oven to 450°F.
2. Season chicken liberally, including cavity, with salt and pepper.
3. Heat 1 Tablespoon oil in cast iron skillet over medium high heat.
4. Use a pair of tongs to hold the whole chicken and sear the chicken as evenly as possible on all sides (about 3 minutes per side).
5. Place chicken on a plate while keeping the skillet warm.
6. Swirl in remaining oil and add all the vegetables plus the zest.
7. Spread out into an even layer and season with salt and pepper.
8. Nestle chicken, breast-side up, over vegetables.

9. Place in oven and let roast until browned and juices run clear (about 35 minutes; internal temperature of thickest thigh part at 165°F).
10. Transfer chicken to chopping board and let rest for 10 minutes before carving.
11. Spoon pan juices over chicken and roasted veggies and serve with lime wedges.

Nutrition (per serving)
Calories 312
Carbs 6 g
Fat 21 g
Protein 23 g
Sodium 97 mg

Roast Harissa Chicken in Schmaltz

Serves: 4
Preparation Time: 15 minutes plus 4 hours brining and 1 hour marinating time
Cooking Time: 45–55 minutes

Ingredients

1 4-pound chicken, halved, backbone and ribcage removed, legs and thighs intact
1 cup three-chili harissa
¼ cup schmaltz (chicken fat) or olive oil

Brine:
8 cups water
1 cup kosher salt, plus more
⅓ cup sugar
3 garlic cloves, smashed, peeled
¼ cup coriander seeds
1 cup ice

Directions

1. Prepare brine. Fill a large pot with the water and stir in salt and sugar until dissolved. Add garlic and coriander and bring mixture to a boil. Remove from heat and add ice. Bring down to room temperature and refrigerate. Brine should be completely cooled before adding the chicken.
2. Submerge chicken halves completely in brine. Cover and let soak, refrigerated, for 1–4 hours (no longer than 12 hours).
3. Remove from brine and rinse. Pat dry, as thoroughly as possible, with paper towels, picking out coriander seeds.
4. Place chicken on a tray or pan. Spread harissa all over chicken, cover tightly and chill for 1 hour to overnight.
5. Preheat oven to 400°F.

6. Heat schmaltz in cast-iron skillet over medium heat.
7. Place chicken halves in skillet, skin-sides in schmaltz.
8. Cook until skin is darkened and beginning to crisp (about 5 minutes).
9. Place in oven and let roast for 25 minutes.
10. Flip chicken over and continue roasting (about 9–12 minutes, internal temperature of thickest thigh part at 165°F).
11. Place chicken on serving dish, skin-side up, with pan juices.

Nutrition (per serving)
Calories 1251
Carbs 23 g
Fat 87 g
Protein 91 g
Sodium 1350 mg

Easy Sriracha-Lime Chicken

Serves: 4
Preparation Time: 5 minutes plus 1 hour marinating time
Cooking Time: 30 minutes

Ingredients
6 chicken thighs, boneless
Salt and pepper, to taste
¼ cup extra virgin olive oil
Juice of 1 lime
½ large onion, sliced
1 Tablespoon Sriracha sauce
Fresh cilantro, chopped, for garnish
½ lime, sliced very thinly (optional)

Directions
1. Pat chicken dry with paper towels.
2. Combine all ingredients, except cilantro, in a Ziploc bag or shallow container.
3. Let marinate, refrigerated, for 1 hour.
4. Preheat oven to 400°F.
5. Transfer chicken and marinade to cast iron skillet, spreading chicken in one layer.
6. Spoon some marinade over chicken.
7. Bake 25 minutes and then transfer to top rack to broil until brown and crisp (about 3–5 minutes).
8. Sprinkle with cilantro and garnish with lime slices (if using).

Nutrition (per serving)
Calories 208
Carbs 2.5 g
Fat 16.4 g
Protein 12.5 g
Sodium 246 mg

Vegetarian Recipes

Potato-Rosemary Flatbreads

Serves: 6
Preparation Time: 20 minutes
Cooking Time: 9–11 minutes

Ingredients

1 large russet potato, scrubbed and unpeeled
2 Tablespoons butter
½ cup plus 2 Tablespoons all-purpose flour, plus more for dusting
1 teaspoon fresh rosemary, finely chopped
1 teaspoon baking powder
1 large egg, lightly beaten
¼ cup finely shredded Manchego or Parmesan cheese
2 Tablespoons buttermilk or milk
2 Tablespoons extra-virgin olive oil or canola oil, divided

Directions

1. Prick potato several times with a fork and cook in the microwave until easily pierced through up to the center with a fork or small knife (about 5 minutes). Let cool.
2. Split in half. Scoop out flesh and transfer to a bowl.
3. Add butter and mash until smooth.
4. Stir in flour, rosemary, baking powder and salt.
5. Add egg, cheese and buttermilk, stirring briefly to combine.
6. Dust hands with flour and shape mixture into a ball.
7. Pat and flatten into a ¼-inch thick circle (about 9½-inch diameter).
8. Dust a knife and cut to make 6 wedges.
9. Heat cast iron skillet over medium heat and swirl in 1 Tablespoon oil.

10. When oil begins to shimmer, put in 3 wedges and cook until browned and puffed (about 2–3 minutes on each side).
11. Place on a sheet of foil and fold edges over to cover.
12. Do the same for the remaining oil and 3 wedges.
13. Serve warm.

Nutrition (per serving)
Calories 198
Carbs 21 g
Fat 10 g
Protein 5 g
Sodium 211 mg

Roasted Japanese Squash with Quinoa and Mushrooms

Serves: 2–4
Preparation Time: 5 minutes
Cooking Time: 30 minutes

Ingredients
4 cups kabocha or Japanese squash, cubed
5 sprigs lemon thyme, divided
2–4 Tablespoons olive oil, divided
Sea salt, to taste
Freshly ground pepper, to taste
5 shallots, sliced
2 garlic cloves, minced
2 cups mushrooms, roughly chopped
Juice of 1 lemon, divided
4 sprigs marjoram, stems removed
1 cup cooked quinoa
Micro tatsoi or spinach mustard, to top

Directions
1. Preheat oven to 375°F. Line a sheet pan with foil.
2. Place kabocha and 3 sprigs of lemon thyme on sheet pan. Drizzle with 2 Tablespoons olive oil and season with salt and pepper. Toss to coat and spread into a single layer. Bake until kabocha are browned and tender (about 30 minutes).
3. Meanwhile, heat remaining oil in cast iron skillet over medium heat. Sauté shallots and garlic until tender and fragrant (about 5 minutes). Add mushrooms and cook until browned (about 5 minutes).

4. Add juice of half a lemon, 2 sprigs lemon thyme, marjoram and quinoa. Stir and cook until herbs are wilted and fragrant (about 3 minutes). Season with salt and pepper and remove from heat.
5. Assemble on a serving dish starting with the roasted kabocha, followed by the mushroom-quinoa mixture and topped with the micro tatsoi.
6. Squeeze remaining lemon juice over mixture and season with salt and pepper.
7. Serve.

Nutrition (per serving)
Calories 286
Carbs 42 g
Fat 10.1 g
Protein 10 g
Sodium 25 mg

Mushroom Paella

Serves: 4–6
Preparation Time: 15 minutes
Cooking Time: 55 minutes

Ingredients
1½ pounds mushrooms of choice (like button, cremini/baby bella, and rehydrated porcini; or combination), stemmed and cut in similar sizes
3 Tablespoons olive oil, divided
1 Tablespoon chopped fresh parsley, plus more for garnish
1 red bell pepper, cored, seeded, and julienned
1 teaspoon sea salt, or to taste
1 medium red onion, sliced thinly
4 cloves garlic, minced
1 teaspoon smoked paprika, or to taste
1 14-ounce can diced tomatoes, undrained
1 14-ounce can artichoke hearts, drained and quartered
2 cups uncooked Arborio rice
4 cups low-sodium vegetable broth
1 cup filtered water
1 teaspoon saffron threads (optional) or ½ teaspoon turmeric
2 lemons, one halved and the other cut into wedges

Directions
1. Heat a 12-inch cast iron skillet over high heat.
2. If using porcini, rehydrate by soaking in boiling water for 15 minutes and then draining off liquid. Set aside.
3. Add mushrooms (except porcini, if using) and reduce heat to medium high.
4. Cook mushrooms until their moisture is released (about 6–8 minutes), stirring constantly for even browning.
5. When mixture looks golden, reduce heat to medium low.

6. Add 1 Tablespoon oil, rehydrated porcini (if using), and parsley.
7. Sautee until parsley is wilted (about 2 minutes).
8. Transfer mushroom mixture to a plate. Raise heat to medium.
9. Using same skillet, add remaining oil, bell pepper, and salt. Sauté until bell pepper is tender and fragrant (about 4 minutes).
10. Add onion and continue cooking to soften (about 3 minutes).
11. Add paprika and garlic and cook to caramelize (about 1 minute).
12. Next, add artichokes and cook until soft (about 2 minutes).
13. Add rice and stir while cooking until grains start to turn translucent (about 1 minute).
14. Stir in broth, water and saffron or turmeric, making sure to wet all the rice.
15. Allow rice to cook (do not cover or stir!) until it begins to absorb liquid (about 10 minutes).
16. Stir in mushrooms and let cook until rice is fluffy and tender (about 10 minutes). Rice should have formed a crust at the bottom of the skillet at this point.
17. Raise heat to high to toast crusted rice at bottom of pan (about 30 seconds). As soon as you smell toasted rice, remove immediately from heat.
18. Cover with foil and let rest for 10 minutes.
19. Drizzle with juice of 1 lemon and sprinkle with parsley and more salt (as needed).
20. Serve immediately with lemon wedges.

Nutrition (per serving)
Calories 344
Carbs 60.1 g
Fat 7.6 g
Protein 8.7 g
Sodium 824 mg

Skillet Pesto Pizza

Serves: 4
Preparation Time: 15 minutes
Cooking Time: 15 minutes

Ingredients
Pizza dough, store bought or homemade
1 Tablespoon extra virgin olive oil
1 cup shredded mozzarella
½ large zucchini, sliced thinly
½ cup ricotta
Red pepper flakes, for garnish

Pesto:
2 cups fresh basil leaves, packed
¼ cup walnuts
¼ cup shelled pistachios
¼ cup grated parmesan cheese
2 Tablespoons Nakano Basil and Oregano Seasoned Rice Vinegar
Salt and pepper, to taste
⅓ cup extra virgin olive oil
1 Tablespoon water (optional)

Directions
1. Prepare pesto. Place all ingredients except olive oil and water (if needed) into a blender or food processor. Pulse briefly to chop. Add olive oil in a thin stream. Process, scraping down sides while adding oil, to get an oily paste. If too thick, thin down with water, added a little at a time. Reserve 2 Tablespoons for drizzling over cooked pizza (if needed, add a few drops water or Nakano Basil and Oregano Rice Vinegar to thin out for easy drizzling). The rest of the pesto for the dough should have a thicker consistency.

2. Preheat oven to 500°F.
3. Coat a 12-inch cast iron skillet with oil.
4. Place the pizza dough in the skillet, patting it so that the diameter is a little larger than that of the bottom of the skillet.
5. Spread pesto over dough, starting from the center and spreading in a circular motion towards the edge. Leave about ½ inch of the edge free.
6. Sprinkle with mozzarella.
7. Arrange zucchini slices on top.
8. Add ricotta in dollops and then sprinkle with red pepper flakes.
9. Place skillet over high heat on stovetop. Cook until you see oil bubbling up the edges of the dough (about 3 minutes).
10. Place in oven and bake until crisp and browned at the edges (about 10–12 minutes).
11. Remove from oven and let sit for 5 minutes in skillet.
12. Transfer to serving plate, drizzle with reserved pesto and cut into wedges.
13. Serve.

Nutrition (per serving)
Calories 550
Carbs 32.6 g
Fat 38.6 g
Protein 18 g
Sodium 1074 mg

Garlic-Turmeric Falafel

Serves: 6–8
Preparation Time: 10 minutes
Cooking Time: 20–25 minutes

Ingredients

Chickpea fritters:
1 flax egg (1 Tablespoon flaxseed meal + 2½ Tablespoons water, left to sit 15 minutes)
1–3 Tablespoons olive oil, divided
4 cloves garlic, minced
½ cup panko bread crumbs
¼ cup fresh parsley, finely chopped
3 Tablespoons vegan parmesan cheese
1 Tablespoon hulled white sesame or hemp seeds
2 teaspoons coconut sugar
½ teaspoon turmeric
1½ teaspoons cumin
Juice of ½ lemon
Sea salt and black pepper, to taste
1 15-ounce can chickpeas, drained, rinsed and dried thoroughly

For Coating:
2 Tablespoons vegan parmesan cheese
3 Tablespoons panko bread crumbs

Directions

1. Add flax egg to a food processor or blender. Set aside while preparing other ingredients.
2. Heat cast iron skillet over medium heat and swirl in 1 Tablespoon olive oil.
3. Sauté minced garlic until slightly browned (about 3 minutes). Let it cool down and then add to flax egg in food processor.

4. Add next 8 ingredients (through lemon juice) to flax egg and garlic, along with about a pinch each of salt and pepper, and 1 teaspoon olive oil.
5. Pulse to break into small bits.
6. Add chickpeas and pulse until mealy in consistency (not too paste-like) and moldable. Adjust flavor, according to taste, with salt, pepper or coconut sugar. Add more panko if mixture is too wet.
7. Mix coating ingredients in a bowl or shallow container.
8. At this point, preheat oven to 375°F and line a baking sheet with aluminum foil.
9. Reheat same cast iron skillet over medium heat. Swirl in enough oil to coat the bottom of the skillet.
10. Use 1 heaping Tablespoon of chickpea mixture to form a ball. Roll in coating mixture and place on a plate or tray (or drop immediately in heated, oiled cast iron skillet). Repeat until mixture is used up. Makes about 16 balls or falafel.
11. Cook, shaking or slanting the pan slightly to roll the falafels, until evenly browned (about 4 minutes total).
12. Arrange the browned falafels in lined baking sheet and bake in preheated oven until golden brown (about 12–15 minutes).
13. Let cool (about 5 minutes) before serving.
14. To serve, top pita or lettuce wraps with desired number of fritters (2–3), fresh tomato, onion, parsley, and sauce.

Nutrition (per serving)
Calories 152
Carbs 15.8 g
Fat 8.4 g
Protein 4.4 g
Sodium 192 mg

Mushroom and Barley Pilaf

Serves: 4
Preparation Time: 15 minutes
Cooking Time: 50 minutes

Ingredients

½ cup dried porcini mushrooms
1 cup boiling water
2 Tablespoons olive oil, divided
7 cups chopped button mushrooms
½ cup dry white wine
⅛ teaspoon black pepper
2 cloves garlic, minced
1 cup onion, chopped finely
2¼ cups water
1 cup pearl barley, uncooked
½ teaspoon salt
¼ cup fresh parsley, chopped
1 Tablespoon butter

Directions

1. Rehydrate porcini mushrooms by soaking in boiling water for 15 minutes. Drain, reserving liquid. Chop finely and set aside.
2. Place about half (3½ cups) of button mushrooms on chopping board and rough chop. Slice those remaining and set aside for later.
3. Heat cast iron skillet over high heat with 1 Tablespoon oil.
4. Sauté chopped button mushrooms until browned (about 5 minutes).
5. Reduce heat to medium and stir in porcini, wine, pepper and garlic. Cook for about 1 minute, just to dry liquid, and remove from heat.

6. In a large saucepan, add remaining oil and onion. Cook until onions are translucent (about 3–5 minutes).
7. Pour in liquid from porcini, water, barley, salt and mushroom mixture. Bring to a boil, cover and reduce heat. Let simmer until barley is tender (about 35 minutes). Add parsley and fluff mixture with a fork.
8. Wipe cast iron skillet clean and add butter. Place over high heat to melt butter. Sauté sliced mushrooms until browned (about 5 minutes), reducing heat if needed.
9. Garnish the barley mixture (pilaf) with sautéed mushroom and serve.

Nutrition (per serving)
Calories 322
Carbs 51.7 g
Fat 10.8 g
Protein 8.4 g
Sodium 338 mg

Lo Mein with Tofu

Serves: 4
Preparation Time: 5 minutes plus 30 minutes pressing time
Cooking Time: 15–20 minutes

Ingredients

1 14-ounce package firm tofu, drained
8 ounces whole-wheat linguine, cooked al dente, according to packaging instructions
1 teaspoon dark sesame oil
½ teaspoon salt, divided
Freshly ground black pepper, to taste
2 Tablespoons canola oil, divided
¾ cup onion, vertically sliced
½ medium head cabbage, shredded
2 medium carrots, peeled, thinly sliced diagonally
2 large cloves garlic, sliced
3 Tablespoons oyster sauce
1½ Tablespoons mirin
1½ Tablespoons less-sodium soy sauce
1 teaspoon rice vinegar
1½ cups bean sprouts
Green onions, chopped, for garnish

Directions

1. Wrap tofu with thick layers of paper towels and press down with a weight or with the cast iron skillet. Let sit for 30 minutes.
2. In a bowl, toss cooked pasta in sesame oil, ¼ teaspoon salt and pepper. Coat well and set aside.
3. Unwrap tofu and wipe off any moisture on the surface. Cut crosswise into 4 large pieces. Season well with remaining salt and pepper.

4. Heat cast iron skillet over medium heat. Swirl in 1 Tablespoon oil.
5. Cook tofu until evenly browned (about 4 minutes on each side). Remove from skillet and cut into bite size pieces. Set aside.
6. Add remaining oil to skillet and sauté onion for 2 minutes.
7. Add cabbage, carrot and garlic and sauté until cabbage wilts.
8. Stir in oyster sauce, mirin, soy sauce and vinegar.
9. Add pasta and bean sprouts.
10. Toss to coat everything well and cook until heated through (about 2 minutes).
11. Sprinkle with green onions and serve.

Nutrition (per serving)
Calories 397
Carbs 55.1 g
Fat 15.4 g
Protein 18.2 g
Sodium 736 mg

Vegetable Samosas with Cilantro-Mint Chutney

Serves: 4–6
Preparation Time: 30 minutes
Cooking Time: 15 minutes

Ingredients
10 egg roll wrappers
1 large egg, lightly beaten
Cooking spray

Chutney:
½ cup fresh cilantro leaves
½ cup fresh mint leaves
¼ cup red onion, chopped
2 Tablespoons fresh lemon juice
1 Tablespoon water
¼ teaspoon kosher salt
⅛ teaspoon sugar
1 serrano chili, chopped coarsely
2 teaspoons fresh ginger, grated or minced

Samosas:
1¼ cups mashed potatoes
¼ cup yellow lentils, cooked
1 Tablespoon fresh mint, minced
1 teaspoon Madras curry powder
1 teaspoon butter, softened
¼ teaspoon kosher salt
¼ teaspoon ground cumin
½ cup frozen petite green peas, thawed

Directions

1. Prepare chutney by placing chutney ingredients in a blender and making a smooth paste. Set aside.
2. Make the filling by combining mashed potatoes, lentils, mint curry powder, butter, salt, and cumin. Mix well. Add peas last and stir in gently.
3. Use one egg roll wrapper at a time (cover the rest with a towel so they don't dry up). Cut in half, lengthwise. You'll have 2 rectangles. Moisten edges with egg. Place 1 Tablespoon of filling near either the top or bottom edge. Take a corner of the wrapper close to the filling and fold it over, making a triangular shape. Continue folding over up to the end of the wrapper. Moisten with more egg, if needed, to seal.
4. Repeat with the rest of the filling and wrappers.
5. Heat cast iron pan over medium-high heat and spray with cooking spray.
6. Coat the samosas lightly with cooking spray as well.
7. Cook samosas until browned (about 1 minute on each side).
8. Serve with chutney.

Nutrition (per serving)

Calories 288
Carbs 58.3 g
Fat 2.6 g
Protein 11 g
Sodium 574 mg

Vegetable Stir Fry

Serves: 7
Preparation Time: 10 minutes
Cooking Time: 10 minutes

Ingredients
⅓ cup plus 2 Tablespoons teriyaki sauce, store-bought or homemade
12 ounces green beans, trimmed
1 small red bell pepper, seeded and cut into thin strips
1 small yellow onion, cut into thin wedges
½ cup carrots, julienned
2 cups shiitake mushrooms, sliced
1 Tablespoon vegetable oil
⅓ cup unsalted cashew nuts

Directions
1. Reserve 2 Tablespoons teriyaki sauce for later.
2. In a large bowl, toss ingredients in ⅓ cup sauce.
3. Heat oil in cast iron skillet over medium high heat.
4. Stir in cashew nuts and cook until fragrant and toasted (about 30 seconds). Remove from skillet and set aside.
5. Stir fry vegetables until slightly charred (about 5 minutes)
6. Stir in reserved sauce, cooking 2 minutes longer.
7. Remove from heat and stir in toasted cashews.
8. Serve.

Nutrition (per serving)
Calories 130
Carbs 16 g
Fat 6 g
Protein 3 g
Sodium 580 mg

Charred Summer Vegetables

Serves: 6
Preparation Time: 10 minutes
Cooking Time: 5 minutes

Ingredients
Cooking spray
2½ cups corn kernels
2 cups green beans, chopped
1 cup zucchini, chopped
1 cup red bell pepper, chopped
2 Tablespoons shallots, finely chopped
1 Tablespoon fresh flat-leaf parsley, chopped
2 Tablespoons fresh lemon juice
4 teaspoons extra virgin olive oil
½ teaspoon fresh thyme, chopped
Salt and pepper, to taste

Directions
1. Heat cast iron skillet over high heat and coat with cooking spray.
2. Add first 4 ingredients (through red bell pepper) to skillet and stir.
3. Cover and let cook for 5 minutes.
4. Meanwhile, combine remaining ingredients well in a bowl.
5. Add to cast iron, tossing well to coat.

Nutrition (per serving)
Calories 102
Carbs 18.5 g
Fat 3.2 g
Protein 3.3 g
Sodium 210 mg

Dessert Recipes

Cranberry Upside-Down Cake

Serves: 10
Preparation Time: 30 minutes
Cooking Time: 30–40 minutes

Ingredients
2 large eggs, separated
¾ cup whole-wheat pastry flour
¾ cup all-purpose flour
2 teaspoons baking powder
¼ teaspoon salt
¾ cup packed light brown sugar
4 Tablespoons unsalted butter, softened, divided
2 Tablespoons plus ¼ cup fresh orange juice, divided
3 cups cranberries
⅓ cup canola oil
1 cup granulated sugar
1 teaspoon vanilla extract
½ cup low-fat milk, at room temperature
Whipped cream, for garnish

Directions
1. Preheat oven to 350°F.
2. Place the egg yolks in a large bowl and the whites in a clean, dry, grease-free bowl. Let sit to bring to room temperature.
3. In a bowl, combine flours, baking powder and salt. Set aside.
4. To cast iron skillet, add brown sugar, 2 Tablespoons butter and 2 Tablespoons orange juice. Heat over medium heat, stirring continuously, until mixture begins to bubble. Immediately remove from heat and let cool.
5. Spray the sides of the cast iron skillet with cooking spray.

115

6. In a sauce pan, add remaining orange juice and cranberries. Bring to a simmer and cook, with stirring, until cranberries burst. In a circular motion, pour into the butter mixture in the skillet.
7. Add remaining butter, oil, granulated sugar and vanilla to yolks. Beat with a mixer at high speed until light colored. Reduce speed and add small amounts of the flour mixture alternately with milk. Do not overmix.
8. Using clean, dry and oil-free beaters, beat egg whites at medium speed until soft peaks form. Pour a third of egg whites into the egg yolk mixture, folding gently. Pour in the rest, folding until uniform in color.
9. Pour batter over cranberry mixture in skillet and spread with a spatula.
10. Bake until golden brown and edges separate from the skillet (about 30–40 minutes).
11. Remove from oven and place skillet on a rack. Let rest for 15 minutes.
12. Loosen sides with a knife and carefully flip skillet over serving plate.
13. Let cool for 30 minutes.
14. Serve with whipped cream.

Nutrition (per serving)
Calories 356
Carbs 56 g
Fat 13 g
Protein 4 g
Sodium 182 mg

Blueberry-Peach Brown Butter Crumble

Serves: 8
Preparation Time: 15 minutes plus 30 minutes freezing time
Cooking Time: 40–45 minutes

Ingredients
Streusel:
1 stick unsalted butter, cut into 4 pieces
½ cup flour
½ cup brown sugar
1 teaspoon ground cinnamon
¾ cup oats

Filling:
4 medium peaches, peeled, pitted and sliced
1 cup blueberries
¼ cup all-purpose flour
¼ cup granulated sugar
¼ teaspoon salt
½ teaspoon vanilla extract

Directions
1. Prepare browned butter. Warm a stainless steel pan over medium heat and add the butter pieces. Swirl with whisk as butter melts. Be careful not to burn the butter. Swirl the pan, if needed. The butter will begin to foam. Continue stirring. Butter will develop a golden hue, with a nutty aroma and dark specks at the bottom (about 5 minutes). Immediately remove from heat and pour into a heat-proof container. Cover and put in freezer to solidify (about 30 minutes).
2. Meanwhile, combine all the other streusel ingredients in a bowl and set aside.

3. Preheat oven to 350°F and grease or spray cast iron skillet.
4. Mix filling ingredients together and spread evenly inside skillet.
5. To the streusel ingredients, add the solidified browned butter and break with a pastry cutter. Mix together to distribute butter until mixture looks crumbly.
6. Sprinkle and spread over filling.
7. Bake until topping is golden brown and filling bubbles (about 40–45 minutes).
8. Remove from oven and place on a rack to cool slightly before serving.

Nutrition (per serving)
Calories 273
Carbs 39.2g
Fat 12.4 g
Protein 3.2 g
Sodium 159 mg

Apple Cobbler

Serves: 10
Preparation Time: 15 minutes
Cooking Time: 1 hour

Ingredients

Filling:
½ cup all-purpose flour
4 pounds Fuji apples, peeled and sliced thinly
⅓ cup sugar
2 Tablespoons butter
2 teaspoons vanilla extract
½ teaspoon salt
½ teaspoon ground cinnamon
¼ teaspoon ground nutmeg
½ cup water

Topping:
1 cup flour
⅓ cup sugar
¼ teaspoon salt
2 teaspoons baking powder
¼ cup chilled butter, cut into small pieces
1 cup low-fat buttermilk

Directions

1. Preheat oven to 375°F.
2. Combine ingredients for filling, mixing well, and place in cast iron skillet.
3. In a bowl, combine dry ingredients for topping (flour, sugar, salt and baking powder). Cut in butter with pastry cutter, fork or two butter knives (or your hands), until mixture looks like coarse meal. Quickly stir in buttermilk to moisten mixture (do not overmix).

4. Cover filling evenly with topping.
5. Bake until topping is golden brown and filling bubbles (about 1 hour).
6. Let cool slightly before serving.

Nutrition (per serving)
Calories 257
Carbs 46.1 g
Fat 7.4 g
Protein 3.2 g
Sodium 349 mg

Apple Upside-Down Cake

Serves: 10
Preparation Time: 25 minutes
Cooking Time: 35 minutes

Ingredients
Topping:
Cooking spray
¾ cup sugar
¼ cup water
2 large Rome apples, sliced ¼ inch thick
¼ cup walnuts, chopped

Cake:
1⅓ cups cake flour
1½ teaspoons baking powder
¼ teaspoon salt
⅔ cup sugar
3 Tablespoons butter, softened
2 large egg yolks
1 teaspoon vanilla extract
½ cup 1% low-fat milk
3 large egg whites, placed in a dry, grease-free bowl

Directions
1. Preheat oven to 350°F.
2. Prepare the topping. Combine sugar and water in a stainless steel sauce pan and heat over medium heat. Swirl slightly to mix, but refrain from overmixing. Cook until sugar dissolves and solution turns golden brown (about 4 minutes). Pour immediately into cast iron skillet. Tip skillet to spread the syrup and coat the bottom evenly. Arrange the apple slices in the syrup (use tongs if syrup is still hot) and sprinkle with nuts. Set aside.

3. Prepare batter for cake. In a medium bowl, combine flour, baking powder and salt. In a large bowl, add sugar and butter. Beat with a mixer at medium speed until light-colored and fluffy. Add egg yolks and vanilla, and beat to combine. Add a small amount of flour mixture and stir, followed by milk, stirring again. Repeat, adding flour mixture alternately with milk.
4. Using clean, dry and oil-free beaters, beat egg whites at high speed until stiff peaks form.
5. Fold egg whites into batter.
6. Pour batter into skillet over apples and spread evenly with a spatula.
7. Bake for 35 minutes or until toothpick inserted in center comes out clean.
8. Remove from oven and place on rack to cool for 5 minutes.
9. Loosen edges using a knife and carefully invert over a serving plate.

Nutrition (per serving)
Calories 253
Carbs 45.8 g
Fat 6.6 g
Protein 3.9 g
Sodium 163 mg

Chocolate Chip Dutch Baby with Banana in Kahlua Syrup

Serves: 6
Preparation Time: 15 minutes
Cooking Time: 12 minutes

Ingredients
¾ cup 2% reduced-fat milk
½ cup all-purpose flour
2 Tablespoons sugar
¼ teaspoon salt
2 large eggs
2 Tablespoons butter, divided
⅓ cup semisweet chocolate chips
3 large firm bananas, halved lengthwise
½ cup Kahlúa
½ cup frozen reduced-calorie whipped topping, thawed

Directions
1. Preheat oven to 450°F.
2. Place cast iron skillet in preheated oven and heat for about 15 minutes.
3. While heating skillet, combine first 5 ingredients (through eggs) in a bowl and whisk until smooth.
4. Swirl 1 Tablespoon butter in the heated skillet to melt and coat.
5. Pour in batter and sprinkle with chocolate chips.
6. Bake until puffed and browned (about 10 minutes). Remove from heat.
7. Make banana in Kahlua. Cut banana halves in half. Melt remaining butter in a saucepan or skillet over medium high heat. Cook banana in butter until browned (2 minutes on each side). Add Kahlua and simmer to impart flavor.

8. Serve Dutch baby topped with banana mixture and whipped topping.

Nutrition (per serving)
Calories 326
Carbs 47.8 g
Fat 10 g
Protein 5.3 g
Sodium 175 mg

Mixed-Berry Grunt

Serves: 8
Preparation Time: 10 minutes
Cooking Time: 25–35 minutes

Ingredients
Filling:
2 pounds fresh mixed berries, such as blueberries, raspberries, and blackberries
¼ cup sugar
2 Tablespoons water
1 Tablespoon fresh lemon juice

Topping:
1 cup all-purpose flour
2 Tablespoons sugar
1 teaspoon baking powder
½ teaspoon baking soda
¼ teaspoon coarse salt
½ cup plus 2 Tablespoons low-fat buttermilk
2 Tablespoons unsalted butter, melted

Cinnamon sugar:
⅛ teaspoon ground cinnamon
1 teaspoon sugar

Directions
1. Put filling ingredients in cast iron skillet and heat over medium high heat. Cook, with occasional stirring, until thickened (about 15 minutes). Remove from heat.
2. In a large bowl, whisk together dry ingredients for topping, then add buttermilk and butter. Mix to form a moist dough.
3. Drop the dough over the berries in 6–8 large dollops.

4. Combine ingredients for cinnamon sugar and sprinkle over the dough.
5. Cover with lid or parchment (pan lining) paper, fitted well, and cook over medium heat until topping is dry and cooked through while filling is bubbly (about 10–20 minutes).

Nutrition (per serving)
Calories 190
Carbs 38 g
Fat 3.7 g
Protein 3.3g
Sodium 163 mg

Pumpkin Cake with Butterscotch Glaze

Serves: 10
Preparation Time: 20 minutes
Cooking Time: 45 minutes

Ingredients
Cake:
¾ cup salted butter, softened
1½ cups granulated sugar
3 large eggs
1 teaspoon vanilla extract
¾ cup pumpkin puree, unsweetened
1 cup white whole wheat flour
½ cup all-purpose flour
1 teaspoon baking powder
½ teaspoon salt
½ teaspoon ground cinnamon
¼ teaspoon ground nutmeg
⅛ teaspoon ground cloves
⅓ cup buttermilk

Glaze:
2 cups powdered sugar, sifted
½ cup caramel syrup
1 Tablespoon milk, or as needed

Directions
1. Preheat the oven to 350.
2. Butter cast iron skillet.
3. Prepare wet ingredients. Place butter and sugar in a large mixing bowl and beat with a mixer until creamed. Add eggs, vanilla and pumpkin and mix together well.
4. Prepare dry ingredients. Combine flours, baking powder, salt, and spices in a bowl.

5. Add dry ingredients to wet ingredients and mix well.
6. Add buttermilk and mix until smooth.
7. Pour batter into buttered skillet, scraping sides of the bowl and spreading with a spatula.
8. Bake until fragrant and set (about 40–45 minutes). Toothpick inserted in center should come out clean.
9. Remove from oven and place skillet on rack to cool.
10. While cake is cooling, prepare glaze. Combine glaze ingredients in a bowl and whisk until smooth. If mixture is too thick, add milk by the teaspoonful to adjust consistency.
11. Drizzle over cake while in skillet or drizzle over individual slices upon serving.

Nutrition (per serving)

Calories 356
Carbs 51.7 g
Fat 15.7 g
Protein 4.9 g
Sodium 170 mg

Chocolate Strawberry German Pancake

Serves: 4
Preparation Time: 15 minutes
Cooking Time: 25 minutes

Ingredients
2 Tablespoons butter, unsalted
⅔ cup whole wheat flour
¼ cup cocoa powder
2 Tablespoons sugar
½ teaspoon salt
1 cup milk
½ teaspoon vanilla extract
4 eggs
Toppings (optional): fruit, confectioners' sugar, chocolate or strawberry syrup, whipped cream

Strawberry mixture:
1 cup strawberries, sliced
1 Tablespoon butter, unsalted
1 Tablespoon honey

Directions
1. Preheat oven to 400°F.
2. Place cast iron pan in oven and heat for 15 minutes.
3. Place butter in heated skillet and swirl to melt and coat (including sides of skillet). Set aside.
4. Prepare batter. In a large bowl, whisk together flour, cocoa powder, sugar, salt, milk and vanilla until smooth. Add eggs and whisk until smooth.
5. Prepare strawberry mixture. Combine ingredients in a saucepan and heat over medium heat. Stir while cooking until syrupy in consistency (about 10 minutes).
6. Pour batter into buttered skillet and spread with a spatula.

7. Spoon strawberry mixture over batter, spreading as evenly as possible.
8. Bake until center of pancake is set (about 20–25 minutes).
9. Serve warm with toppings (if desired)

Nutrition (per serving)
Calories 327
Carbs 40.5 g
Fat 14.8 g
Protein 12.4 g
Sodium 397 mg

Plum Clafoutis

Serves: 6
Preparation Time: 20 minutes
Cooking Time: 60 minutes

Ingredients
1 Tablespoon unsalted butter, softened
6 to 8 medium plums, cut into ¼-inch wedges
⅔ cup granulated sugar, divided
½ cup unbleached all-purpose flour
¼ teaspoon fine sea salt
4 eggs
1½ cups whole milk
1 Tablespoon vanilla extract
Confectioners' sugar

Directions
1. Heat the oven to 350°F. Set rack to center of oven.
2. Place empty cast iron pan in oven and heat for 15 minutes.
3. Use mitten to remove cast iron skillet from oven and coat with softened butter (including sides).
4. Coat plum wedges with ⅓ cup of sugar and arrange in skillet.
5. In a bowl, combine sugar, flour and salt. Whisk in eggs and then add milk and vanilla. Whisk to combine.
6. Pour batter over plums.
7. Bake until set (about 1 hour).
8. Remove from heat and let cool.
9. Slice and serve dusted with confectioners' sugar.

Nutrition (per serving)
Calories 270
Carbs 45 g
Fat 7 g
Protein 7 g
Sodium 165 mg

Recipe Index

Also by Louise Davidson

Here are some of Louise Davidson's other cookbooks.

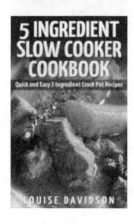

Appendix – Cooking Conversion Charts

1. Measuring Equivalent Chart

Type	Imperial	Imperial	Metric
Weight	1 dry ounce		28g
	1 pound	16 dry ounces	0.45 kg
Volume	1 teaspoon		5 ml
	1 dessert spoon	2 teaspoons	10 ml
	1 tablespoon	3 teaspoons	15 ml
	1 Australian tablespoon	4 teaspoons	20 ml
	1 fluid ounce	2 tablespoons	30 ml
	1 cup	16 tablespoons	240 ml
	1 cup	8 fluid ounces	240 ml
	1 pint	2 cups	470 ml
	1 quart	2 pints	0.95 l
	1 gallon	4 quarts	3.8 l
Length	1 inch		2.54 cm

* Numbers are rounded to the closest equivalent

2. Oven Temperature Equivalent Chart

Fahrenheit (°F)	Celsius (°C)	Gas Mark
220	100	
225	110	1/4
250	120	1/2
275	140	1
300	150	2
325	160	3
350	180	4
375	190	5
400	200	6
425	220	7
450	230	8
475	250	9
500	260	

* Celsius(°C) = [T(°F)-32] * 5/9

** Fahrenheit (°F) = T(°C) * 9/5 + 32

*** Numbers are rounded to the closest equivalent

Made in the USA
Coppell, TX
08 July 2024

34417540R00079